MOVING TRUTH(S)

Queer and Transgender Writings on Family

with

Aparajeeta 'Sasha' Duttchoudhury and Rukie Hartman

Flying Chickadee

ISBN 978-0-9896263-5-4

First printing, April 2015

Flying Chickadee

www.flyingchickadee.com

Inquiries and interest in curating process and creative content may be directed to movingtruths@gmail.com

Original ornamental art for cover by Rukie Hartman

Cover Design, book Design and editorial guidance by Shirin Subhani and Shahana Dattagupta of Flying Chickadee

Contents

Preface

"When we face pain in relationships our first response is often to sever bonds rather than to maintain commitment."

— Bell Hooks, *All About Love: New Visions*

For those of us who call ourselves "Desi" or "South Asian" in the diaspora, living outside of our homelands, there is often a need to find community. We trace our histories through South Asia and our migrations and/or families' migrations that have relocated us all over the world. Though the details of our migrations are different, they bring us together to form relationships rooted in similarity. We act as a community and when we meet other South Asians, there is often a Desire to socialize, to make sure the kids know each other, to celebrate holidays, and concern ourselves with the politics of the lands we left behind. Our intergenerational bonds allow us to balance keeping our cultures alive and fitting into an environment that, we perceive, sees us as different.

In Desi communities, because we have worked hard to create safety nets of familiarity, sometimes our differences can deeply affect our relationships with one another, especially within families. LGBQ (Lesbian, Gay, Bisexual, Queer) and Transgender South Asians often face stigmas associated with their sexuality and gender, which can be a source of pain for both the individual and the family. Shame and guilt are the driving forces behind this pain. Often LGBQ and Transgender Desis receive messages that their sexuality and gender are not right because these aren't seen or acknowledged within Desi culture, further intensifying an experience of disconnection between cultural /familial / ancestral and sexual / gender experiences.

When we get to a point where we are exploring our gender and sexuality and realize our experiences don't match the expectations we have been taught to embody, we tend to gravitate toward popular LGBQ and Transgender justice movements. This can be hurtful for our families because we are seen as moving away from our people and our culture, and toward a community in which our families do not see themselves reflected. Though these justice movements can help us feel validated in our gender and sexuality, we also feel the impact of familial disconnect because these movements do not actively address family relationships and how to shift together with them. This means that our families aren't being given many opportunities to learn more about their LGBQ or Transgender family members in a way that is culturally relevant.

This shared pain and the limitations of most justice movements make sharing our stories as LGBQ and/or Transgender South Asians with and about family difficult. As facilitators of this anthology, we see allyship as a key part of mending and growing relationships with our families. Allyship in the context of this book is about us as LGBQ and Transgender South Asians telling our stories in hopes that our families and community can learn more about us, that we may all reconcile any pain we have collectively experienced and set forth a new foundation for understanding each other better. This anthology aims to be an honest and kind allyship resource for our families and for each other.

Introduction:
Everyone Needs an Anu Aunty

Sasha Duttchoudhury and Rukie Hartman

Relationships founded on storytelling can be the most exciting and the most frightening relationships in which we can find ourselves. They offer moments of reflection and growth, which, in the case of Anu meant being pushed to ask questions when we thought we already had the facts. The sneaky danger, and beauty, of befriending an English professor lie in experiencing seemingly mundane interactions that blossom with insight. Even before getting to know her, Anu taught us that facts are really questions in disguise. For someone who might be mistaken as "just another aunty" because of her small build and modest attire, Anu soon revealed herself to be a radical, compassionate, powerhouse. She exemplified so much of what we feared and admired about exploring stories as Desis in the diaspora, and eagerly, we grew in her presence. Though we both met Anu in different contexts, each of us was equally and powerfully transformed by our storytelling relationships with Anu.

It is through stories, in the form of art, poetry, dance, music, and other forms of creative expression, that the humanities explore human cultures, allowing students to unravel the mysteries that are ourselves and each other. As LGBQ (Lesbian, Gay, Bisexual, Queer) and Transgender Desis whose stories are often absent from our experiences of culture and community, the humanities became a place where we had the opportunity to fill these voids with our own stories. Before taking a class with Anu, we took many humanities classes where we had explored our stories alongside feminist theory. There was a sense of comfort, justice, and solidarity in this space where our stories were wanted instead of dismissed. It was here, too, that our efforts to find and tell our stories became grounds for competition; hard-lined stories about who is more privileged or who is most marginalized surfaced instead of simply an evolving or temporary space to learn more about each other's experiences. Theory overshadowed storytelling and sharing, and we got swept up in it.

As students in the humanities who had built up a bit of an academic ego, we came to Anu fully equipped to critique and analyze, but not entirely prepared to listen and grow. Our academic and social justice ventures had taught us all about the atrocities humans have committed against each other, and we had learned to see harm and injustice in everything. We had picked up this keen sense from like-minded academics, who also thought they knew the facts. Pointing out issues that are "problematic" became a routine in which we'd smoothly cite theory, quote feminist writers, and arrive at a logical conclusion proving our claim. We were comfortable in this routine and it was with this ease and confidence that we would dismiss others who did not follow our logic. The behavior that came with this new academic "knowledge" pushed us away from the inspiration with which we pursued the humanities in the first place. Ironically, we came into the humanities to share our stories, but then weren't willing to let others learn from or about us.

When it came to family, this was especially difficult. We had learned to understand ourselves in such complicated terms and through such daunting concepts that talking to family was sometimes unfulfilling. In a world where talking about identities is difficult enough, communicating who we are, as we continue to understand it ourselves, to those most dear to us now seemed practically impossible. We finally had a way to communicate and understand ourselves with peers who shared our academic language and critical thinking perspective. It was easy to lean on the idea that our families just wouldn't understand who we are. It seems fair to say we made a wrong assumption because we weren't yet ready to explore how we could help our families understand.

Anu's classes made the discrepancy between our original intentions and our actual practices very clear. Though we were hesitant to shift from our rigid and self-righteous ways at first, Anu's patience and generosity made a deep and lasting impact on our thinking. In her classes, we were challenged in the kindest ways; we were encouraged to be more gentle, to slow down, to breathe, to celebrate and to engage where we would have previously shut down. Anu was more than familiar with all the theory we knew. She knew about the ugliness in the world, she knew about stories heard and unheard, and she knew that there were more fulfilling ways to think about these issues. Anu used kindness, inquiry and exploration to remind us of the humanity in the stories we read and shared. She urged us to see possible connections between seemingly unrelated ideas, including our sexualities, our genders, our ethnicities and our families. Her ability to hear our stories with an openness that recognized both our pain as well as our joy modeled for us new ways to practice justice through telling and receiving stories. Sharing our stories became about learning how to extend care to others and to the relationships in between.

In Anu's classes, critical thinking and talking about issues of justice also became a creative endeavor. In one class, she asked us how we knew what we knew, not to question our knowledge, but to help us better trace our own thinking. In another class, she asked us to comment on a film we'd watched and to respond as if the filmmaker were in the room, as a way to practice kind critical thinking. Once we were asked to explain a theoretical concept to a young person in our lives, so that we could step away from academic jargon and communicate big ideas more simply. She'd say "queer" out loud and ask our class to think about queerness which initially made us giggle but also underlined her allyship. To have another South Asian welcome these identities felt bold; she was using her classroom as a medium to extend care, to acknowledge and invite these stories into the room. Maybe this is what led us to trust her so much. As Queer South Asians who are invested in social justice, our paths of *who we are* and *how we want to be*, became illuminated. We didn't try to seek singular answers or rely on the same sets of theory to make our point. We looked for the goodness, for the multiple views of right and wrong, and for ways to engage with love and care.

It was this generous lens that brought us to (and we bring to) this anthology. Now able to see in multiple dimensions and be open to other dimensions yet unseen, the need for us to step up as allies to foster our Desi communities from whom we seek support and understanding has become pertinent. Anu's friendship and mentorship have helped us see that this includes mending relationships with family, community, and ourselves. She has offered us the space to ground our approach in love, and grow the necessary skills to act in a loving way. Connecting with a group of LGBQ and Transgender Desis who wish to approach family with grace, to process pain and to transform family relationships through our stories, became an important part of our own healing. We have wanted to put together an anthology for LGBQ and Transgender Desis for a long time. The generosity and growth catalyzed in us by Anu have allowed us to address the topic of family with the profound care and responsibility it deserves. Through her influence we were able to connect with Flying Chickadee, our fabulous publishers, and South Asian Americans Leading Together (SAALT), the organization supporting this project through the 2014 Young Leaders Institute (YLI).

The emotional and practical structure of this project has been driven by allowing our questions to guide the process: Would there be people who would want to write about their family with a focus on allyship? Are we equipped to support people in writing about family? Will our stories create a balanced narrative about our experiences with family? Our relationship with Anu has not only flourished but has also helped us build more storytelling relationships with other Desis. The vulnerability and openness these relationships take to kindle are often rare, but when you find yourself in moments like this, the magic of such relationships is palpable.

Our journey with this project has left us believing that everyone needs an Anu Aunty.

1

The Picture Beyond the Frame

Rajat Singh

This isn't a coming-out story. It's a "coming-in" story, an invitation within the frame, into new kinds of home and family.

The apartment I share with my boyfriend is decorated with photographs of the two of us, scattered across crowded bookshelves and walls painted elephant-grey. Our eyes in each picture hold the gaze of the onlooker: they stare back at those who celebrate the happiness we share in each photo. When family comes over, we can either put the photos away, or we can display them, and let the smiles in the photographs intimate to our dear ones stories of our sweet memories. Our smiles are material reminders that at that very moment of a camera flashing, we were happy. Perhaps because we were together, perhaps because we were surrounded with loved ones – or perhaps because, in our hearts, we knew that this photograph would travel and reveal its subjects' happiness to anyone who looked upon it.

* * *

My nerves were firing all over the place as I struggled to ready my home for their visit. I hadn't eaten breakfast that day, too nervous to get anything down and too worried about creating more work for me to clean up. I spent the morning scrubbing every surface of my one-bedroom apartment, and snapping at my boyfriend, Nikhil, not a few times to stay out of my way.

"You can't just leave your stuff there – are you going to pick that up – can you help – no, just don't bother." The tension was building and I had no place else to release it except onto the closest body that would take it.

My dad parked the car on my tree-lined block on West Seventy-Third Street, just as I was running out to pick up essentials from the bodega, like cereal, milk and flowers. And of course, there had to be wine on hand. My parents don't drink that much, but since I didn't know their preferences, I'd bought too much. I would end up drinking most of it.

My parents, who live in Boston, don't make me anxious, and I love them immensely. But this was their first visit to New York staying at my apartment that I shared with Nikhil. That weekend, they had been invited to a wedding in the city. Their decision to stay with me was financial, no doubt, but it had deeper, more emotional implications. As much as I was apprehensive about what might happen, I secretly wanted to go to that place of discomfort. I needed all of us to go there as a group, to break some of the *politesse*, and to enter a space from where it wouldn't be possible to turn around.

I'm not sure what I was expecting, or how to articulate what I wanted to happen. It's frustrating to think that some of us don't have the language to describe the pictures of family that we want to imagine, but that inevitably exist outside our experience. When words cannot be spoken, some feelings seem almost impossible. But this essay suggests new ways that, confronted with the limits of language, we can reframe the conventions of what we think of and accept as "family."

* * *

My mother had broached the subject with me weeks earlier while visiting me on her own. We were sitting in my Nani's room at her nursing home in Flushing, the faint beep of a machine next to her bed making its presence rudely felt. I reflected nostalgically on the fact that, after my Nana passed and his apartment was rented to strangers, my parents' visits to New York had become fewer and more riddled with tension. My mother had been displaced in a very new way, and I felt helpless to ease her feelings of disconnection.

In many ways, I am the good Indian son, and yet I have disappointed my parents on many occasions. Since starting graduate work, my parents have been helping me financially, which has made me more conscious of what filial obligations mean and how they manifest themselves materially. "I couldn't turn away the very people who were paying for my place," I scoffed, imagining that an American would surely tell his parents to stay in a hotel.

Two years earlier, I had told my parents that Nikhil and I were living together, a fact that certainly took them time to come to terms with. And now, I welcomed my parents into Nikhil's and my apartment without a second thought. But a part of me also secretly wanted the four of us to get closer, to share new experiences, and to engage with scary and uncomfortable emotions.

That Saturday in April, my parents arrived, bearing gifts and Tupperware filled with home-cooked Punjabi fare. My dad even contributed a bottle of red and one of white, and I blushed, thinking of how silly I had been, running errands and rushing to get everything that I thought we might need for a weekend of potential awkwardness. The secret joy (and misfortune) of parents is that sometimes they know what you need better than you do.

* * *

I remember how, when I was a child, my mother had kept a drawer of old *dupattas*. These were the head-scarves that no longer belonged to a Punjabi *salwar-kameez*, or had become frayed, or out of fashion. They weren't suitable for wearing out in public on Saturday evenings to fancy dinner-parties. But I gaily appropriated her cast-offs. Some were unfortunately garish in color or pattern, and I never played with those, but I certainly did have my favorites. The *dupattas* weren't for me, and yet I was given access to their mystical powers.

They were both fetish and fantasy, allowing me a way to materially explore a world that was denied to me. I danced to my favorite 90s Bollywood item-numbers, tying the *dupattas* into elaborate configurations across my body, mimicking the hip-thrusts and sultry moves that constituted my steady diet of Hindi movies.

In this private world created just for me, fantasies became animated, away from the judgmental *nazar* of strangers and aunties' raised eyebrows. I can't recall any photographs of "dress-up" time having been taken when I was young. Such a material reminder would have made guests, who took sight of them in my home's many photo albums, feel an invasive pleasure in viewing my innermost Desires. And I would have been left with a hot burn of shame in my body, prickling my insides.

Some parents know you better than you know yourself. I can't imagine how painful it was for them to see those moments of playtime realized in their son, and I can't imagine how painful it was for them to make allowances for it.

Their son was so pretty.

* * *

At the time of my parents' visit, Nikhil and I had been together for four years. This wasn't the first time they were meeting him. Nikhil was in his last months of medical school, and I was halfway through my Master's program. He was everything my parents envisioned I would be – handsome, respectful, intelligent. And a future doctor, no less. I thought that graduate school would in some way redeem me in their eyes for the fragile promise I implicitly broke when I told them I was gay.

Both of them immigrants from India, my parents met and married hastily. Sometimes I'm too afraid to ask them why they chose one another, or whether difficult circumstances and fears enjoined them to one another. My parents share a quiet closeness between them, something like what Mira Jacob calls a "karmic trade-off." Their marriage wasn't arranged, yet it has spoken to me as tinged with a quiet indifference. They have shown me what honest love looks like, as well as silent longing.

They settled in Boston, raising me and my younger sister Rachel to live humbly. Our apartment was small. My upbringing conditioned me to take up less space in the world than I feel I deserve. I wanted things. I still do. My parents pushed Rachel and me to pursue ambitious careers – professions they themselves couldn't pursue. For them, these careers meant an entrée into worlds from which they didn't want us excluded. Growing up, we lived at the margins of our doctor-friends' lives, Indians who had left the *desh* for a piece of that cookie-cutter American dream: a chance at happiness and a big house in the suburbs.

Nayan Shah writes of the tension queer Indian-Americans have to reconcile between cultural and familial bonds, along with notions of dependence, as they butt against dominant Western notions that privilege the independence of the individual. But coming out means different things to everyone, and the constraints that bind each of us commit us to sometimes-contradictory political projects.

As I wrote earlier: this isn't a coming-out story. It's a "coming-in," an invitation within the frame, into new kinds of home and family.

I made the decision to tell my parents I was gay, several years earlier, in large part because Nikhil had become so important in my life. Inviting my parents to stay with us, in my imagination, would mean a new sense of homecoming. Our New York apartment that weekend wasn't just a place to stay, but the space in which an emerging family would grow together. Together, we would remember those bittersweet pasts that had brought us here, painful histories of 1947 and uneasy struggles to acclimate to strange and lonely new lands halfway around the world in the 1980s. And together we would imagine that our futures didn't seem so impossible when my parents saw their *beta* happy. Even his love, outside the constraints of their experience, wouldn't seem so impossible.

* * *

Nikhil came home right around tea-time – a 5PM ritual never missed at my parents' home. Home now seemed to be anywhere they could have their quotidian traditions. Fully caffeinated, they dressed in the bedroom. Their Indian outfits were sophisticated and distinctly *not* showy.

The Picture Beyond the Frame

My mother has never worn Designer *saris* (I've tried to encourage her into purchasing a few), her tastes always veering on the side of stylish but not flashy. Her mother, after all, is famous for having great taste. I won't inherit any of the gold jewelry for my demure, wheatish-complexioned wife. But I did manage to steal our family's aesthetic flair.

My mother's Soir de Paris perfume wafted across the room, stirring memories in me of my parents dressing for parties when I was a child. She hand-selected the gold jewelry that would match just right. My father poured himself a Scotch before leaving the house, which I never developed a taste for, but always appreciated its rich, amber warmth. This was a dance choreographed over years of intimate familiarity with one another.

Their stylized rituals girded them to face a roomful of shallow Indian-Americans, those with the big-shot careers, whose children lived in Manhattan, like me, but weren't scholars or queer: their sons were self-important investment bankers and their daughters were marriageable and ready to meet me.

My mother wore her characteristic giddiness (that masked an inner nervousness). Dad wore a naturally calm and collected air, but he was excitedly talking to Nikhil and getting directions from him – to dictate to the cab-driver, no less. My mother glided out of the bedroom in a marigold and magenta chiffon *sari*, her slender fingers reaching for a velvet clutch that matched my father's onyx-black silk *achhkan*.

Nikhil offered to take a picture of the both of them, and I could sense my mother's nerves flutter. An almost undetectable ripple of tension broke the fragilely constructed frame of our weekend. The intimacy of our weekend together, as four members of a delicately budding family, would be made distinctly visible in the material reminder of a photograph. From that moment onward, nothing would be the same.

I didn't offer to shoot them – instead it was Nikhil. Maybe he was just being nice. Or maybe he was overstepping. But either way, he was part of a new family. Nikhil wasn't even in the picture, but in an unseen way, he *was* the picture.

Roland Barthes writes that the "blind field" is that which exists outside the frame, beyond the photograph's edges. The borders index "something already there," yet unseen. What are the conditions that have allowed a photograph to be taken? Who captured the moment? What do we remember outside of the material reminder, and what was left out? What exists at the margins if you shift the lens slightly? This, to use Ann Stoler's words, demands "a different kind of attention to the familiar and the strange, to both what is singular and significant, and to what is intentionally askew and out of place." And what within the frame pricks us? What about Nikhil's picture of my parents stays with me?

Taking someone's picture is a personal act, charged with intimacy and trust. Nikhil was let into a seemingly unremarkable moment, but his presence became an eruption. The material reminder of his intervention is the photograph that he subsequently retouched, printed, and framed for my parents' wedding anniversary gift a month later. The photograph captured their smiles at a moment when they were anticipating their night on the town, sure. But I like to imagine that they smiled thinking about the new forms of family they were coming to terms with.

Nikhil's photograph of Mom and Dad called on us all to rediscover the burgeoning articulations of a new family, of a new allyship. Characteristically unassuming and polite, Nikhil made little imposition, never asking me to tell my parents about him, and never asking for more space in my life than he thought I would be comfortable sharing with him. This weekend just happened to be the one time I did ask for more space.

There was a silent acknowledgement that rippled through the room and clicked with the flash of the iPhone that evening.

It's a well-accepted notion that diasporic South Asian families don't talk. We sweep under the carpet those very uncomfortable or unthinkable admissions of personal struggle and interpersonal conflict, thereby perpetuating cultures of power that silence nonconforming voices, stories, and experiences. But what would it look like to question a culture of silence, and examine less visible forms of communication, openness, and allyship within Indian families, which may perhaps be couched in the shadows? At what point do faint glimmers of allyship emerge, and how do we know how and when to spot the inchoate?

* * *

Like some stubborn snail, I've burdened my body with a sedimentary and sentimental history of guilt and anxiety. I have had little success letting go of old pains, deep fears that my life has found paths so unimaginable to my parents' aspirations for me. That it has found expressions of happiness through languages so untranslatable to them. My wounded self tells me there are things in life that I don't have a right to claim for myself, and I continue to heed their prohibitions.

Perhaps my guilt stems from those inconvenient suspicions that the love I grew up with has been a challenged version of something else that I imagined my parents could have for one another. I carry with me the love my parents have shown my sister and me. I have been luckier than many queer people who are close to me. My parents have allowed their children to create futures for themselves that are liberated from their own histories. New homes bring new loves.

I've never been told that I wasn't wanted, that I would be disowned, or that I didn't belong. Even still, I've internalized strong pressures to please my parents, hiding missteps and insecurities from them along the way. But my parents' coming to the U.S. has allowed them to imagine a future for a love that is not so impossible. I can live a life that I chose.

For I love freely.

2

A Dent in the Universe

Sasha Duttchoudhury

Baba has always had a way of reminding me how special I am when I'm feeling discouraged or inadequate. "Do you know who you are?" he asks earnestly, excitedly and rhetorically. He reminds me what my name means; Aparajeeta, *"someone who cannot be defeated."* He tells me I am the only Aparajeeta Duttchoudhury in the whole world, in the history of the world. The only "me" there ever was and ever will be. He recounts all the ways the universe had to conspire to give me life. He brings together science, philosophy and spirituality, to show me how slim chances came to fruition for me: life on Earth, the random collision of asteroids and the creation of the moon. It all happened for me. Baba says the space-time continuum exists for me! He says that I am the force that navigated the lives of my ancestors. Every moment in the lives of every one of my ancestors were magnetized to fall into place just for me. People had to be born, classes had to be skipped, exams had to be passed or failed, trains had to be caught or missed, people had to be married, scholarships had to be awarded or denied, migrations had to have been journeyed whether by force or choice, people had to have survived, mistakes had to have been made... all so that I could exist as me. He says that *this* is how special I am, and that this is how much the universe loves me. And this power to create planets, life, family histories, to create circumstance and coincidence, is within me. He says I hold the power to mold the world, to create myself. Baba says *this* is who I am: an incarnation of the universe.

I used to think Baba was being dramatic because I had a more mundane mental image of myself: a static product of adventure. How could I be the glamorous being Baba thought I was if I couldn't even live up to the expectations I inherited? As the child of parents who spanned the planet for the chance of better opportunities, I existed as a dream long before I was born. When my parents imagined their first born child, they didn't think of someone like me. They must have imagined someone bold like themselves. Someone who could more fully honor the immigrant dream of "a better life" that brought them to the United States. And yet here I am, powerful, undefeatable, and nothing like what my parents expected. Deeply sentimental bleeding hearts don't climb the corporate ladder. Urban foodies don't make authentic *aloo gobi* without bowing to the temptation of experimentation. Sci-fi nerds don't outgrow their commitment to unworldly knowledge. Second generation children of immigrants don't major in English and dream of writing books for a living. Young Desi girls don't fall in love with Shahrukh Khan *and* aspire to be like him — funny, charming, and sensitive — to complicate the dashed lines that define friendship and intimacy, or to challenge tradition in the name of love in the way he has bravely and dramatically shown we can. Young Desi girls don't teach their fathers about love and philosophy.

Despite my transgressions, Baba and I have more in common than ever: short hair, short stature, glasses, and an affinity for darker colors in our wardrobe. We have the same nose and the same sense of humor. Baba and I are also amateur philosophers. Maa sighs at our lengthy discussions on semantics and epistemology, modern derivations of ancient teachings. She teases us, blaming Bengali blood for what she sees as over-intellectual and useless conversation, and wonders where her Punjabi audacity manifests in me. As if insisting I love both parents equally, I assure Maa that part of her is in me too.

While it is all in good fun, I can see where I begin to peel away from the carbon paper that is Baba. It amazes me how his existential questions and his engineering practicality can inhabit a single mind. I would listen to his ideas with wide eyes and awe before I could configure my own. It took years for me to unhinge myself from the orbit of his thoughts to nurture my own curiosity, ask my own questions, and seek my own answers. Though I, too, am ignited by inquiry, this is where we differ. In this phase of exploration I couldn't find clear answers the way Baba did. He is certain of who he is and who he is not. With him everything is always absolutely clear. Maybe this is because he is an engineer, and he lives his life based on hard facts. Or maybe this was a trait that blossomed with age. What was uncertain, though, was why I am not like that and why there was so much in-betweenness for me. Somehow my life has put me in places of both or neither, and while this way of being was often uncomfortable because we live in a world that prides itself on discrete definition, these fuzzy lines are where I exist. Few of the questions I ask about myself provide definitive answers, and this is where I find both possibility and panic. Whereas, Baba finds strength in structure and safety in certainty. He seeks out questions and conquers them with answers. This is his adventure. It was my adventure too, until I realized that questions don't always have answers in the way we imagine. Some questions do not have answers, while others have more than one answer. Yet others need not be answered at all. And depending on the question being asked, some of those answers can be extremely painful.

Baba often asks me if I am happy. In the fraction of the second it takes for me to say my predictable, "yes," I calculate the consequences of the answer instead of seeking the truth. Would Baba feel bad if I said, "no"? He might feel bad about himself as a father. He might blame himself for my answer. I might make him feel bad. Wouldn't Baba be happier if I said, "yes"? I wonder if Baba feels this anxiety when he so effortlessly answers questions. I wanted to give him the certainty he found comfort in. I used to struggle to delve into the questions he asked because I was more concerned with the immediate consequences than with the ultimate consequences: a moment of truth. Even now, I occasionally find myself seeking the "right" answer over the answer I know to be true. This constant conflict between the truth of fact and the comfort of fiction could only stem from over-thinking, which leaves me feeling baseless and afraid to confront the actual question. I was never any good at giving answers.

When Baba found out I was dating a girl, he asked, "How do you know you love her?" I had no answer for him. How do I answer this? I retreated into the comfort of silence. There is no answer for this, not in English, certainly not in Bangla or Hindi, not in words at all. My gut reaction was to apologize, for I had neither given him the truth nor the comfort of an answer he wanted to hear. The knots in my stomach had risen to my throat.

I wonder if Baba remembers his lessons about "who I am" when we talk about queerness. When he cried over my short haircut, did he still believe I was a grand manifestation of the universe? Or were his words just sweet nothings to cheer me up? Does he see that queerness is a part of his lessons on who I am? Could "who I am" be all that he says I am, including my queerness? I want to tell Baba in his philosophical speak, "Maybe if you remember who you say I am, you will see how relative this is in the grand scheme of things! We've spent hours talking about who we are beyond form, this body and how we are seen and understood according to this world! If only you could remember the perspective you used to give me, you would remember that I am still me!" I want him to see how my queerness is an integral aspect of the cosmic being he says I am, so maybe we both can ground our relationship in the connection we have as the only "Baba" and the only "Rani Maa" in the history of the world.

While my queerness matters very much, the way it has shaken up our relationship is not necessarily a testament to the significance of my queerness alone. "Queer" is a word I learned to use to communicate something about me in the context of society and culture, it is relative to the society around me. It isn't me at the core, but something about me in this moment. The realization of my queerness and the realization of myself as a piece of the universe don't compare: one is worldly and sociological, and the other is simply spiritual. I imagined he of all people would recognize this. So why the big fuss? Why the doubt and disappointment? Especially when understanding who I am in the context of society has given me the foundation of openness to eventually begin understanding who I am in the context of the universe. I wish I been able to express this to him in the moment, but I was also feeling his pain. I imagine him feeling hurt when he realizes the comfort I gave him was false. But, would he sense the fear behind that decision? Behind every silent and convenient answer I gave him to questions he dreaded asking? On one hand I hold truth and on the other, I hold the expectation of comfort, the fruit of seed I planted long ago. I ache under the weight of it. He grits his teeth, saying things we both wish he hadn't, and I know he is aching too. He too is battling what is in front of him and what is expected of him.

Maa has been a silent spectator, but now, when needed most she chimes in, "When you love someone... you just know." I think she understands or feels something close to understanding. For her, this is a matter of knowing beyond intellect. It is just true and there is no argument because this truth is known and felt on a deeper, wordless level. I am confused, happy, and crying still. Whenever I'm shaken into confronting reality in its rawest, least processed form, I feel dazed, dizzy, and dumbfounded. There is no time to comprehend what just happened. All I can do is be and breathe. And feel grateful. Maybe this is growth. Maybe I'm one of the lucky ones. I'd done everything in my power to avoid confronting what I thought was the truth of how my family relates to my queerness. I'd extrapolated, assumed, and contorted ungrounded logic to fall into line with stories I'd heard from queer Desi friends; there is no happy ending for us. But maybe Maa's rescue was proof that I could invest a little bit of faith in the potential for growth toward acceptance? Maybe I could expect more from them than anger and disappointment. Was this a sign that we could be the Desi family lucky enough to survive, and possibly thrive in having a queer child?

Maa and Baba look at each other. Baba is silent for the first time in an hour. Intellect cannot win here. The philosopher is stumped. The father is questioned. The tension dissipates. We all breathe and I think we all want to laugh a little. It is so simple!

The universe bent over backwards for Baba to confront the complexity of his own question, and to be enlightened to the fact that sometimes "just knowing" is answer enough. Scientific studies, statistics, engineering samples, none of these could speak to his question in the way feeling or a sense could. This confrontation my parents had with my queerness breathed truth into us, putting on the kitchen table its masterpiece – what some might call "dirty laundry." Even still, truth is a painful pill to swallow. When we are surprised to find that "logical" answers don't always exist, we get scared, angry, confused, hurt and disappointed. Embracing my queerness taught me to embrace a way of knowing that comes more from the gut than from the mind. Confronting my truth has not been as intellectual as it has been spiritual, it has been about recognizing that who I am is not something the mind can understand. And likewise, I cannot expect such clear-cut lines from the world around me. It takes a lot of openness to nurture the unknown, unprocessed and uncategorized, to welcome the discomfort of questions unanswered. It takes a different kind of boldness to know answers through the gut than from the mind when the mind doesn't want to see what is really there. It must take a genius of the heart to know these truths, and to be patient enough with others to help them grow into this truth.

For every ounce of intelligence and wisdom my Baba holds, he holds just as much resistance, anxiety and fear. Sometimes my human Baba needs comforting too. He needs a reminder that I am okay in the way that fathers need reassurance that their children are okay. I want to remind him that the care the universe took to put me together doesn't ever warrant an apology. I try to be patient with him, like he was patient with me when I was younger. I try to remember that just like the universe, he put a lot of love into caring for me, his Rani Maa. I try to remember that philosophers are always learning, and as partners in inquiry, we are both growing together. I try to be patient with myself, too. I imagine that Baba's anxiety and fear are born out of the conflict between the truth he seeks and the world around him. And it helps neither me nor my parents for me to blame them for not understanding. We are both negotiating subtle teachings and lived experiences, so I teach myself to be patient with the frustration I have with the lies they have been fed about gender and sexuality. I remind myself that Baba just needs time to embrace the gravity of the truths with which he once used to comfort me. He knows who I am, but I think he needs time to accept the fact that all of me is part of the universe's masterpiece, my queerness included. These are moments for both of us to grow as people, as philosophers, and as family. And as philosophers, we grow through our questions.

I still wonder if my parents are proud of me. Baba tells me that pride is rooted in who we are, and who I am is not singular. He says that I am never alone because there are histories of people behind me, in whom I should be proud. I am not just me, but rather, I represent my ancestors who played a part in making me who I am. Baba says everything I do is connected to my lineage, represents them, shames them, or honors them. I'm told grand stories of doctors who saved kings, Punjabi soldiers in the Indian army, engineers with roads named after them, economists and anthropologists with medals, farmers who lived to be 109 years old, Bengali elites for whom I should have pride, the honor that runs through my blood. But I've never heard of ancestors in my lineage like me. I hear less and less about the artists, writers and musicians. I hear less and less about the depressed and anxious. I hear even less about the queer and gender creative; those who challenged what it means to "be a man" or "be a woman." It's as if they never existed. The only blips they hold in the lifeline of our family history are vague and dismissive, "He was a little weird… but his father was really brilliant" or "There isn't much to say about her, but her sister was a real gem!" These ancestors have been hidden and forgotten so effectively. Maybe they were conveniently overshadowed by the doctors and engineers, overlooked by family historians for the sake of being concise or more glamorous. Or maybe for the sake of their own safety, they hid themselves so as to avoid judgment or cultural stigma. We do strange things in the name of honor and pride, hiding ourselves and silencing others. Honor seems to be only given to those who already have the trophy of a story that is eagerly shared. Does honoring your ancestors mean only honoring the ones who are deemed high achievers? Does honor mean reducing ancestors to their achievement, conveniently ignoring the struggle and disappointment it took to achieve? How might we honor our ancestors in a holistic way, accepting all of the truth that comes with our lineage, without evaluation or judgment?

In the way children often are skeptical of their parents, I didn't always believe what Baba told me about me, yet I now know viscerally that he is right. We are both right. I am the universe, truly born of stardust. Baba says that I am here to put a dent in the universe. I take this to mean fully inhabiting my truth, knowing that pretending or choosing to deny myself the truth is what truly dishonors the history and future of our family. The question and power of truth is much larger than the questions of right or wrong, moral or immoral, natural or unnatural. I do represent my ancestors – I embody all of my silenced ancestors, all of the oddballs, the outsiders, the overlooked, and I am honored to do so. The more I allow myself to just be, the more I am able to root myself in truths Baba taught me and to help the people around me see this truth. One day, I will be an ancestor, and I want to be honored for my truths and quirks. I want my descendants to know they too are children of cosmic magic and, just as they are, they put a dent in the universe.

3

Rebirthing Renegades

Alina Bee

There are millions of ways family can break you, some covertly and some not. Stay wary. It's always easier to normalize the hurt than to really feel it. It hurts less when you let it be and just let things happen because sometimes it feels like everything is just vying to screw you over, so why push so hard when you're going to be on your knees in just a matter of time? But feeling hopeless doesn't mean you're weak. Numbing when it gets too much, avoiding it or moving away so you're not constantly confronted by it, is okay. Making art, going to the gym, writing, music, whatever method you choose to cope is fine. It's okay. And if you're not hurting anyone, make no apologies about it, to anyone. If you can find ways that are kind to yourself, that don't bring more hurt into your life, aim for that. You don't have to punish yourself anymore.

You are terrifying

and strange and beautiful

something not everyone knows how to love.

– Warsan Shire, *"For women that are difficult to love"*

Family relationships have been inconsistent and volatile for as long as I can remember. When I was younger I recognized love in its fullest when I was around my paternal grandparents. It was always kind, even in anger or pain. It always felt warm. Most of my other family relationships have been abusive and manipulative. While the words 'love', 'friendship', 'care' and 'support' were often thrown around, I learned the hard way that I couldn't necessarily trust those words so easily. I had to be careful with who I let hurt me and not perpetuate those abusive understandings of love. And it's very recent that I learned how to do that – if only because of the love that my paternal grandparents, Dadu and Daadi Jaan, nurtured me with. They are my reasons for surviving, for loving and allowing myself to be loved. They made me capable of loving bigger than the rest of my family taught me. Their love sheltered me, coached me and made me realize that whoever I was, I was always worth more than the world would have me believe.

Baby Alina

My childhood was spent fluctuating between being acutely aware of how certain feelings I had were problematic and constantly looking for that bigger, accepting love my grandparents raised me with. And honestly, I was only able to have a childhood because of my grandparents. I cannot stress that enough.

As a little girl I always played basketball with the boys, rode my bicycle and skated fast around other girls, refused to hang out with my girl cousins at family parties and wore my hair **short**. Any adornment to my hair was slowly coaxed out with grumbles and pouts until it mysteriously disappeared, never to be found again by Ma. Baba owned a computer repair factory at the time, and I'd bring home all the unusable, burnt-out computer parts. In true little boi fashion, I'd pull them apart with pliers and screwdrivers and hammer them into computer dust, which I would carefully put back into my 'future robot parts' box.

When I was five, I realized that there was something fundamentally dangerous about how I felt and presented, because I felt viscerally uncomfortable in gendered spaces. Gendered groups for activities were common in kindergarten and I always wanted to be on the boys' team. Picture day would come twice a year and I hated wearing the *shalwar kameez* that spotlighted my otherwise indiscernible gender. I wasn't happy playing the damsel in distress; like in the movies I always wanted to be the hero, the one to sweep the girl off her feet with my sweetness, holding my ground when things got rough. You never know when there'd be a sudden need for a strong, dominating figure to defend a girl's honor. And I was ready, in all my brawny, five-year-old glory to be that person.

Or so I thought, until I reached the 5th grade. The neighborhood kids I used to play with asked me if I wanted to be a boy. I told them "no." Something about the way they asked made me feel visible and strange in a way that didn't feel comfortable. One kid called me a dyke. I didn't know what that was. I was fine being called a tom-boi, or covertly being mistaken as a boy, but when I was directly confronted about my gender, it confused me and made me upset. Why did they ask me questions I hadn't even thought about? Why did those questions make me feel like there was something they were looking for? And why did my presence seem to make so many people uncomfortable?

So, mission "Stay Hidden" was in full effect by summer of 6th grade. I took inventory of all my concerning gender traits and realigned themselves with more normative gender traits. I grew out my hair, started wearing more 'feminine' clothes, got contacts, learned what make-up was (kind of) and started making conscious efforts to notice and voice my attraction to boys. I paired my increasing femininity with a pushback against everything that I used to enjoy. I stopped hanging out with my boy cousins and joined in with the girls. I stopped playing with science kits and reading books as much, and started focusing on music, on decorating all my spaces with color and art, and on my appearance.

Appearance became really important to me. Not in a typical coming into yourself type of way, but in a 'how can I make myself physically look more acceptable, so people stop chafing and commenting all the time?' way. It was a lot of self-hate and self-flagellation to consciously push back against myself. There was a running joke between one of my cousins and myself about first impressions. When she first met us in Karachi, I was wearing overalls, a t-shirt and tennis shoes, while Bushra, my younger sister, had on a dress, nail polish, plastic kid heels and a bunch of chunky, colorful plastic jewelry. I was seven. That was one of the first impressions a lot of my family in Karachi had of me, and it basically sums up my whole childhood. T-shirts, jeans, monotone colors, no jewelry (despite having my ears pierced), round coke-bottle glasses, some dirt under my nails, and you got me. 60 pounds of gender-confused, hyper-active, must-protect-all-the-girls, thick-haired brown boi who loved to make *besan ka halwa* and rice krispies, help Ma in the vegetable garden, work on cars with Baba in the garage and hang out with Dadu, building storage sheds in the backyard. I think maybe I was just too much to stomach for my biological family, so the pushback was to make me more digestible for them.

I remember one of the oddly 'feminine' traits I had even in my tom-boihood was a fascination with hair. With cutting, styling, or just taking care of my scalp, I was always into hair. And I had an exasperated

Ma who'd tell anyone that she dreamt of the day I'd let her do something with my hair. I used to style my short hair with gel and baby oil in a bouffant, which really didn't help anyone understand my gender better. I remember feeling really happy with my hair one special day in 4th grade. While walking back to class from recess some kid scrunched up his face and said, "Is that a boy or a girl?" The question wasn't posed to anyone in particular, just a remark for anyone who was close enough to hear it, and for me. I grinned and kept walking but it deflated the happy bubble my hair had going for me and brought that confusion back into focus. When I decided to grow my hair out in attempts to be 'feminine,' I was very insistent on having the best shampoos, scalp therapy conditioners and curl protectors.

Yet even in adopting feminized ways of presenting myself, there were characteristics I could do nothing about, like my strong jaw, broad shoulders and height, which at 5'-3" made me the second tallest in my family. This was used by my sisters a lot – how I was naturally masculine and hulkish because I was bigger than them. My longer hair didn't fit right on my frame. My smile enunciated my jaw. My walk was too hurried and casual, thus manly, or too slow and deliberate, so my effort was too obvious. My newfound femininity was constantly picked at and made to feel even more foreign than it already was. Put up against the femininity of my sisters, who were shorter, thinner, and a lot more acquainted with self-adornment, I felt like I was always at a loss. My masculinity was always obvious, my femininity too awkward to feel or look natural. No amount of hair products, perfume, dresses or boy-crushes could change that.

It didn't matter that in the larger sense, I really wasn't looking for the gendered attention in the first place, and all attempts to address it were because of negative reactions to my unconsciousness about it. I became bent on making myself smaller and hiding in that comfort. My mannerisms – the way I moved, talked, who I interacted with, how I interacted with them, what my clothes, body, perfume and friends looked like and meant to other people – were all in my active consciousness. I hyper-analyzed every movement, desperate to keep hidden the parts of me that were so problematic, and spotlight the new things that I had adopted to be and feel accepted. I was so eager to be loved and to be acknowledged that I would revel in and replay any compliment that came my way and try to embellish that particular trait. I would consciously dissociate from myself and try to push myself into thinking and being like someone else. Someone that was easy to stomach. It was always jarring when I'd be in one of my dissociative states, sometimes for weeks, and I'd catch my reflection in the mirror. I didn't remember or think I looked like I did sometimes because I was too wrapped up in trying to be someone else.

Sustaining all that effort required huge amounts of energy, and when I failed to get acknowledgement for that or it was too short-lived, I tried even harder. It did upset me; I lashed out a lot at my sisters when they highlighted and ridiculed something I was already trying to hide. It wasn't because they didn't know I was insecure about it, they just didn't seem to understand how deeply it hurt. Sometimes they just used my insecurity or my unwillingness to respond with vitriol to win an argument, which hurt more than it angered me, especially if I did respond because then it was suddenly about poor self-control. It was easy for them to maintain dominance when I was riddled with so much shame, guilt, and dysphoria and was always looking to please. I was exhausted all the time and people didn't realize it. I guess it didn't make sense, ya know? How could a kid with virtually no responsibilities aside from homework and a few chores feel *that* depleted?

At the time I didn't have the understanding or words for what the exhaustion stemmed from, but constantly feeling strange within myself was heavy. And boundaries didn't make sense when everything seemed to be fair game to comment, ridicule, praise or talk about. Putting myself first meant I'd have to be okay with keeping certain thoughts and feelings to myself. I'd have to create and stick to my limits even if no one else agreed or joined me. I'd have to enjoy my own company, and I didn't.

Parentals (Content Warnings)

With my parents, there have been multiple up and down periods. Until recently, I had never been verbally communicative of my feelings when my parents would lash out; rather, I'd retreat into my silence and pray for them to stop. I went for years without talking at all to Baba about his anger or emotional distances, the longest being my first two years at college. I had gone for a joy-ride near the house without a license or permit, and he came home early. This wasn't the first time he'd caught me doing this, and he was livid. He choked and hit me until I saw stars, took the lock off my door, took my laptop away and told me that I couldn't go to college, get a job or go anywhere unless he said so. At that time I hadn't spoken to my mom for nearly six months because she had slapped me after I told her that wasn't okay anymore. I was sixteen.

Out of the four of us kids, I bristled and pushed back against the abuse much more vocally. Sometimes I responded non-verbally and I think that upset them the most. Because I was calling on a higher knowledge of self and body that they didn't appreciate, or feel comfortable with me using. My siblings did respond, but not to the point that they stopped talking to our parents or left the house. This has been and continues to be thrown in my face when anyone, meaning my parents, my siblings and their spouses, are mad at me. They would routinely say that I'm difficult, that no one gets along with me, that I think I'm so much better than everyone else. I believed them for a really long time. Sometimes I still do.

When I was younger, my anger was more directed at feeling trivialized and physically hurt for petty reasons. At the time, I didn't understand how the abuse affected my self-image, my mental health, my chances of success or my ability to stay loving and understanding... Years of gaslighting taught me to distrust myself and want to hide every time I felt too visible, even if subconsciously it felt comfortable. Because of the cyclical abuse, my efforts to remain focused on the potential of a different future, one in which I actually truly loved myself and found a balance between success and honesty about where I came from, felt disturbingly idealistic. My repeated efforts to change my circumstances and self-image throughout the years were short-lived and always failed because I was bound either financially, emotionally or physically to my family. They made sure I never forgot that. Every violent confrontation that happened harshly reminded me that no matter how much I tried to change myself and adopt a better understanding of my parents, it wasn't going to break the cycle. After enough times, I stopped trying to push back against it and resigned to the pattern that said, "Escape is impossible. You're not in control of this. You're hardly in control of yourself."

Because of the love I've been blessed to have from recent communities and my grandparents, I was able to survive. And only because of that. They picked me up when I gave up. They told me this was not okay when I truly believed I was unlovable and had tried everything to change myself and my circumstances, except suicide. They taught me. I would not have learned this otherwise.

At this point, I am much more in control of my self-image and am able to weather the flare-ups with distance and emotional apathy. It's hard to not be cynical and spiteful at times. It is also a struggle to maintain a healthy distance because of the guilt of having failed at multiple familial relationships and occasional doubt in the form of, "*Was it really that bad? Am I making too much of it? Is it because my 'American' upbringing has taught me to judge my parents more harshly? I wasn't the only one who was hurt, so why am I unable to let it be and continue on with life? Am I somehow rejecting my culture by no longer trying and hoping for better days with my family? Am I ungrateful because I finally created and stuck to my boundaries?"*

The most upsetting part for me has been that the abuse is still unacknowledged as damaging and that there is no regret for pushing me or my siblings into this emotional distance. For years, I dreamed about the day where I could confront my parents and they'd own up to the damage. For years, they've shown me that this is not probable and increasingly so in recent months. In my feeble attempts at some self-preservation, I learned the language of my father, my mother, my siblings, my communities very well. I tried to speak to them multiple times and they rejected me. I know their language. Even if they deny me, I now know that I tried my hardest. But I still don't know how much blame to attribute to my parents' personal refusal to acknowledge the effect of the abuse and how much to attribute to the normalization of abuse in Desi cultures.

A rose by any other name still has thorns. Abuse is like the elephant in the room for Desis sometimes. It feels oddly like cultural rejection or almost offensive to name it. When discussing the beatings we had with our cousins, we never used the word abuse. Abuse was something white kids claimed; for us, it was just a momentary interruption in our day. Yet abuse is so common in Desi families, it's a whole fucking sketch in Russell Peters' shows. Among other comedians as well. Daadi Jaan would tell me stories about her mother beating her into a daze sometimes and how she made sure never to lay a hand on Ma because of it. But there is no accountability or will to hold her mother accountable for how she hurt her. It just is what it is. I think that naming abuse, calling out the ways we damage each other sets off so many alarms and instigates cultural confrontations that are uncommon. I think there's a need to protect cultural baggage in conversation with other cultures, but at this point I need, and I'm not alone, to have more conversations intra-community about abuse. Because it fucked me up.

The Old Goat and the Young Stallion

As I said before, part of my consistent pushback came from having grandparents who were so consciously loving and attuned to how hurtful and destructive emotional abuse can be for a kid. They didn't use violence as a means of discipline and actively discussed the trauma that came from that. We used to joke that when people become parents, they tend to discipline their kids differently than how they were disciplined. If they were raised in comfort and love, they'd be more likely to lash out when they were stressed because they didn't understand how much that could negatively affect their kids. If they were raised in antagonistic and hurtful environments, they'd try their hardest to keep that away from their kids. Or maybe they felt guilty about continuing the pattern if they did lash out. The joke didn't entirely hold true sometimes, but as a kid it pacified me. It would simultaneously make sense of and minimize the pain of failing familial relationships, discourage resentment and push me to think beyond my own feelings and perception. Sometimes it's easier to think that family doesn't understand, rather than doesn't care.

From my earliest memories, my grandparents had struggled with a variety of chronic health issues. Every moment with them was a little slower, a little sweeter, and a little fuller. They both had highly dynamic lives that felt almost unreal or magical. When they'd tell me stories, I'd sit entranced, alert and attentive, trying to make sure I soaked in every word, every pause, every emotion and try to re-imagine it like it happened. Daadi Jaan told me stories about growing up in Delhi with all in her cousins in their multi-family *haveli*. She would say 'Be bold, frank and of strong character' and tell me about the knots and cooking tricks she learned in

Scouts. Dadu was always the life of the party, in any age group. His wit was incomparable and would often be used to mess with my Daadi. He would crack jokes about how handsome, young and fit he was and how Daadi Jaan was an old goat before he even married her. She once said to him, "You look like a monkey." To which he responded, "So that makes you a she-monkey." Dadu could hold his own in any crowd, any conversation. He managed to infuse undertones of love and caring even in the most heated debates. I don't know anyone, living or dead that was as graceful with it as he was. And I always felt that as great as he was to everyone else, there was a small part of that greatness he saved just for me.

When my grandparents were around, it felt like everything strange about me was or would be okay. Like maybe I didn't have all the answers now and that though people thought all sorts of things about me, I could still be loved. I'd spend the majority of my days when they would visit in a dreamy trance thinking about how much I loved them, and how if I was more like them, I'd be lovable too.

Bringing it in

I became friends with my cousin, Marjaan, in my third year of college. She was the first person who appreciated and celebrated me in all my truths. She was my first real safe space. My grandparents were amazing, but there was much that I could not share with them out of cultural dissonance, respect and concern for the impact that knowing certain things about me could have on their mental health. So Marjaan was really the first person to see me in all my fullness. We would talk about insecurities, family drama, friendship, love, anger, hurt, healing, and she taught me so much by example. Marjaan was the first person whom I felt thoroughly comfortable having over at my house, as much as I was at hers. Granted being family and growing up together definitely helped, but we had a rocky relationship before college, family and all. Marjaan taught me how to keep boundaries between family life, college, partners and friends. She taught me how to navigate shame, guilt, negative self-perceptions and progress with patience and love.

But I was still afraid to tell her about my queerness. I didn't tell her until I was already in a relationship and it was affecting ours because I was always having to hide things from her. I would make excuses for not being able to meet up as frequently, and when I finally did tell her the reason why, it was understandably not the most thrilling news. It explained my behavior a little better, but it still didn't address the fact that I hadn't been a best friend to her for a while, or how dangerous it was being in a queer relationship this close to home. Marjaan finding out about me, changed what I needed from her as family and as a friend. And she rose to the occasion in ways I could not have expected.

She didn't make a big deal out of it. She didn't suddenly excuse herself to go change elsewhere or stop hugging me or change the topics of what she normally talked about with me. She didn't stop talking to me, which I had been preparing myself for. She would casually ask, 'Meet anyone cute today?' or ask what I looked for in a person, without mentioning gender. She was curious but really respectful when asking about my relationship at the time and about sex. Which I could never completely answer because I'd collapse in a fit of giggles, while she'd remain unamused and wait for me to finish. She was so intentional and loving and that radically started changing how I thought about myself and the world around me.

Until I had a physical example present in my life, someone who was unapologetically herself and consciously made space for me, I didn't know what friendship could be. I was so caught up in the appearance of what I thought friendship was without ever bringing it into myself. I always thought friendship or love would be mine in a different version of me. Not in all my fullness. I fundamentally believed that there were parts of me that could not be understood, accepted, loved or healed without anger and force. Until I had someone celebrating me and holding me accountable when I was hurtful /ignoring my responsibilities as a friend, I wasn't growing in any way productive or safe or full. I wasn't accountable to anyone, even myself. I was painfully distrustful of people and flailing but surviving in so much loneliness and toxicity.

In having a friend like Marjaan, I learned how to love people more fully, how to navigate their particularities with attention and love, how to be generous without harsh limits. I learned how to hold people accountable for their damaging words and actions, I learned boundaries, and I learned to put myself and the well-being of those who are kind and grateful before that of those who are cruel. It took having Marjaan in my life to realize what I deserve, and what others deserve from me. And for that I am eternally grateful to God(dess), the cosmos, my grandparents and all the love that held me through unlearning everything that abuse had taught me.

Unbecomings

From my college experiences, I internalized valuable inter- and intrapersonal knowledge. My work as a diversity trainer taught me how to be more attentive to the multiple ways people affect other people's well-being and success. I was introduced to the program by a member who happened to be around when I was performing a piece for an event on global hunger and poverty. I was introduced to concepts like white supremacy, violence and greed, destruction of families, religion, shame and sexuality; all concepts that felt instantly connected to me, but I had never had the names for. Many of my classes so far had been incredibly Euro-centric and had never explored race, gender, sexuality or religions beyond Christianity. In finally having these opportunities, I learned a lot more about accountability and love. Still, I struggled to bring this new energy home or into any space outside of academia.

Until recently, I was only able to understand oppression and abuse from a very academic dynamic. I was unable to make the jump from there to my personal experience until I was out of state for work, with my brother, who is the safest and most comfortable person in my family for me to be around. It was just the two of us for a month, managing work, exploring the city, watching horrible TV and consuming offensive amounts of coffee. It was great. But it was also heavily intertwined with daily confrontations of issues we have with our parents, Appa and her husband, and how we both feel disadvantaged in our overall life successes because of our familial relationships. We'd never had those conversations before; not like that. And in that month, I learned how to negotiate the different understandings I have about self, love, family, Desiness, queerness and community.

How? I still really don't know. I can only say that people are constantly communicating with each other, and it's not always verbal. If you're not talking over someone or are present in their presence, you learn more about yourself than you think. And if you're blessed to have someone that is actively conscious and responsible in the way they affect you, it's revolutionary.

And when they aren't, it's like a time bomb. When things are going well, when my anxiety isn't too bad and work is productive, it's like the abuse never happened and maybe never will, again. My parents are more affectionate, they're kind and they're relaxed, until I feel anxious or overwhelmed by something they don't understand, and the pressure starts building again. All sirens go off and the confrontation of everything I wish I could distance myself from about Baba, Ma and myself becomes a waiting game. But honestly, love, being present, patience, space and calm have always felt conditional. It has always felt like a matter of time before it all goes to shit.

Revealing and reveling

Where I'm at now: The last few college and post-college years have been the biggest learning experiences about my queerness, the violence/demonization/isolation I come from, love/loathing, and BOUNDARIES. I've learned how to put up and feel okay with setting boundaries in the last five months because I've dealt with so much more abuse from my parents and my sisters post-graduation. Part of that is because I'm back at home and working in the family business, so I'm spatially much more involved at home than I've ever been in my life. I'm constantly around my parents without the buffer of school or other activities. And I'm more linked to Appa because of my niece.

It still hurts every time there is a confrontation. Even if it's just verbal now, it instigates a really vivid fight-or-flight sense every time my parents or sisters raise their voices or ask presumptuous questions. I've normalized their behavior, avoided it, fought against it, reasoned with it and it still gets under my skin every time. The thing about cyclical abuse and dysphoria is that it leaves marks that you can't see, erase or build over. If you don't have help or community, two things can generally happen. One, you can develop self-harming coping mechanisms and be continually exhausted from all the energy depleted by negative emotions. Or two, you can normalize the abuse, avoid it, learn to move around it and attempt to dispel the negative emotions that come after a confrontation. You attempt to make space for happiness to recharge from the abuse.

Let me be clear: both are harmful and violent to the soul. Neither can carry and sustain you. Until there is distance from the abuse, until there is conscious help to address and unlearn the coping mechanisms that were adopted, unless there is consistent, unrelenting love that is careful, patient and responsible, the person cannot begin to heal. Abuse is a cycle. Unlearning it means breaking it, recognizing it and learning that it wasn't and isn't okay, making space to deal with all the feelings silenced by normalizing it, and surrounding yourself with love and community to sustain a new, healthier movement.

I can't stress the last part enough. Community is so important. It takes people who will nourish you and help sustain that distance from everything the abuse taught you. It is by far one of the biggest aspects of healing I still struggle with. One of the fundamental points the abuse ingrained in me, is that being true to myself is not okay. It's dangerous. It consistently reminds me that my circumstances can change in a heartbeat if my family knew that I am queer. All this self-love and overcoming trauma still doesn't speak about how unsafe and dangerous it can be to be Desi, queer and not open to family for so many of us. Even now, writing this under a pen name, having more people who know some of my deepest, honest truths, while covering any tracks that could lead to me, I'm still scared out of my mind. I feel reckless being this honest, but if I don't share my story now, I don't know what to do with myself anymore.

The movement

In terms of how the dynamics of family and friends shaped the way I interacted with myself, I had to tell myself regularly that I was and can be emotionally destructive and hurt other people because I was hurting. I couldn't sustain movement any other way, because I was exhausted, because they pushed me too far and didn't understand what they were doing, and I was done trying to explain to people who refused to listen. I felt so much guilt all the time for existing, for being a bad friend, for not having friends with whom I could be honest, for feeling angry or for trying to hold anyone accountable for how they hurt me, because I always felt like somehow in some small way, I had instigated the drama.

One of my friends had a horrible breakup and would text me multiple times a day while I was out of the country, seeking comfort and love. I was more than happy to be there for her, but at that time I was also dealing with intense emotional abuse from Appa, physical abuse and then intentional silence from Baba, and I was also trying to take care of my Daadi, who was being severely neglected by other family. My friend had a lot going on, so I understood the lack of reciprocity in concern for my circumstances. But when I told her I was going through a lot of distress as well, she was dismissive and asked, "Really, mmm, like what? Oh. Okay. That's tough." That one stung more than it made me question myself. I had so many shitty examples of what love, family, allyship and accountability looked like that any attempts at it were short-lived or volatile. I built friendships only to watch them fall apart because of poor allyship on their part and on my part, my own shame, guilt and exhaustion from not being comfortable with myself.

I had to simultaneously learn to forgive myself while holding myself accountable too. Knowing this made me feel that much more desperate for healthy community, often to the point of feeling reckless. I felt like I was spilling everywhere in hopes that by some coincidence I'd find people (or they'd find me) whom I could just *be* with. Part of this stemmed from a personal Desire to not constantly fear negative judgment or abandonment. Maybe they'd truly like me, maybe I'd think they were great too, and our friendship would be productive. I'd become a better me, and maybe it would be a little easier than all the other relationships I had and have in my life. Though, sometimes I still can't believe that it's possible to have this, or that in some ways I do have this. It baffles me to no end. I'll still retreat into myself because I viscerally feel that sharing my incomplete thoughts, feelings and confusions is frustrating, and people won't know what to do. They'll get tired of me, and I'll feel guilty again for being *too much*, *too fast*, *too different* and *too unpredictable*. I'm continuing to learn that a big part of allyship is taking things you don't understand in stride and in love, slowly if you're confused, with patience and space for healthy boundaries.

I continue to realize that allyship in family or chosen family is a process that changes as we change. Sometimes allyship is easily found and felt in family and sometimes it's just you and yourself trying to stay moving through everything else. The biggest thing to stay conscious of is always that you in all your truths and feelings are inherently legitimate and worthy. Your fuck ups don't make you a fuck up, your incomplete aspects don't mean your entire existence is lacking, your particulars or peculiarities don't make you unlovable. It's just always about your process and being hard on yourself or inviting the negative energies in, is counterproductive. You are lovely and good allyship makes you remember it and feel it. There is no room for doubt in your greatness.

Healing myself

One of the biggest issues I've been having lately has been making space for myself – leaving a space if I feel like people are becoming dangerously frustrated, not engaging with their anger or dismissive tendencies – and doing things that make me happy like going to the gym, facials, cooking, exploring the city, etc. Maintaining self-love in my family means keeping all conversations and interactions to-the-point and non-revealing about the details of my life. I've had enough confrontations with family in which being called distant, selfish, strange and continually questioned about my religion, sexuality, loyalty to family and overall lifestyle have become routine. If it doesn't happen every few weeks, I start to anticipate the worst. This behavior has become so expected that I didn't realize how radical it is for me to have this new space.

At this point in my life, I refuse to stop feeling my emotions even when it hurts; especially if it hurts. I'm learning to push myself, on my own terms, and rework the destructive coping mechanisms I adopted before. I hold people accountable but in my family and friends it's not easy, safe or even kind. Sometimes I feel like it's naive, or stupid, and feel apathetic toward my own well-being. Like I know this is going to hurt me but I'm just tired of trying to 'learn' these abusive family dynamics, these reductive social interaction norms, these self-alienating mannerisms. Maybe this is my way of protesting. I don't know if it's self-martyring or if it's radical, I just know it doesn't feel good anymore. I'm continually realizing that I have to make space for myself and simultaneously find and keep good friends around so that I don't resort to my old toxic coping mechanisms again.

I know one quality in myself that's never changed: I am resilient. I go through different experiences and keep thinking that this is it, this is when things change completely and I've finally arrived and it's all going to be easier now. That feeling is short-lived because situations keep repeating themselves. It feels like déjà vu except I anticipate and dread it happening. Still, being so intricately tied in with family feels destructive and demoralizing because I see myself take three steps forward and two to the side. Sometimes I feel like I can move through anything; it's just about perspective and being kinder to myself. But I know that I also refuse to acknowledge the intensity of my depression and anxiety and how it turns into regret and shame. In a sense, it's not a cycle because I am different every time – it's more of a spiral, which still sucks but I know that if I continue taking steps to the side, I might find myself on a different wavelength.

Keeping the self-care consistent is a problem because it requires confronting hurtful memories, and hurtful people who are currently in my life. I also need people or self-care activities that I can lean on when it becomes too overwhelming, but I don't even have energy for the first part, since I am continually in the same environment with the same hurtful people. It's not like I haven't tried but even good friends can feel abrasive when you think you're unlovable. I can't confront the people who've hurt me the worst because they don't hear me and honestly I've been feeling like an open wound the more I try and implement self-care. Distance and time are the only way plausible to heal and address my traumas.

I still feel like I'm looking for home, to be in a space with people who make me feel whole; not overly coddled, not downplayed or exaggerated, not loved from a distance or toxically enmeshed, but loved honestly, warmly and fully. Through perhaps as Warsan Shire said, "At the end of the day, it isn't where I came from. Maybe home is somewhere I'm going and never have been before."

4

The Pensieve

Bish Pleez

He is 21. *He stares at the bottle labels and the names conjure up images of molecules in his head. He remembers that frightful year of organic chemistry required in his training to become a physician.* Benzodiazepines and opioids – what dosage would be required? He looks that up easily on discussion forums, probably inhabited by similarly distraught souls. He confirms the dosage by cross-referencing dosage warnings on PubMed, the medical repository he has often used to conduct research while writing his honors thesis. The phone rings in the background, jarring him back to reality. He ignores it. He needs an escape. An *end*. Nothing seems to be going well, and the future looks bleak. It has been several days since he has been home, but his family has not called him to check if he is okay. "How long will it take them to find out?" he wonders. Days? Weeks? Months? He has felt "low" before but can't remember feeling so hopeless. The blinds on the windows are drawn, the air inside stuffy. He takes in the faded popcorn ceiling, the stained carpet, and the mix of prescription bottles on the desk. "If you leave me I will tell your family you're gay" his boyfriend shouts whilst pounding on the closed door. He threatens to kick the door down yelling, "I am warning you. Your family will disown you. You won't have a place to live or money to finish your college. Only I love you. Without me you are finished." His boyfriend is bigger, older and 'out' as gay. They have been fighting for days; there is verbal, emotional and physical abuse. Or has it been months? He tries to remember but he is exhausted from the cycles of fear and escalation, followed by periods of calm. Today, it has gotten out of hand. He has barricaded himself inside the study in fear. He feels helpless. He is ashamed of feeling helpless. He is in a new country and without any friends who he can trust with his dirty secret: *he sleeps with men*. Society hates him, and he hates himself. When even God is going to smite him down for his sins eventually, why not hasten the process? Even the law decrees him a freak for having "intercourse against the order of nature."

The jangling of the phone shatters the silence again. He reaches to turn it off but fumbles and connects instead. "Hello? Hello? Hello? Were you asleep? It is Ma speaking. Happy Birthday, *beta*! *Kamon aachheesh*, How are you? " she says.

* * *

He is 8. He hates cricket. He is small, severely myopic, clumsy and effeminate. Strangers scare him and the playground is full of them. He doesn't understand the rules of the game or of these social interactions. He doesn't seem to have the necessary hand-eye coordination either. He is getting accustomed to the taunts and jeers of the other boys. They make him much more nervous. One day someone yells "You're a *hijra*!" From then onwards they all take up the chant and sing in high pitched voices filled with the cruelty children often unknowingly inflict upon each other. He does not want to be different. He has to prove them wrong. He certainly does not want to be a *hijra*; the beggars he sees singing and dancing and committing lewd acts for money, on the street. He is very confused by this accusation though – is he one? He looks it up. A textbook in the library informs him that *hijras* are hermaphrodites with male and female parts. The daily humiliation becomes ritualistic, sometimes interspersed with being pushed around. He wants to stay home, but his family wants him to be 'normal' and be a boy, instead of staying home like a "delicate, girly thing." He is forced to leave home every evening for playtime but cannot bear to return to the cricket pitch. He starts hiding out by the field instead and lies about it at home. They find out. He gets dragged to the field and pushed into the fray. "Make him play," his grandmother says. He is called up to bat and the jeering starts. He is trembling and so nervous that he can barely hold the bat between his sweaty palms. The biggest bully is going to 'bowl' against him. He knows he has to hit the ball no matter what. Everything depends on his bat making contact with that ball. His masculinity, his competence, his normality, they all hang in the balance. The bowler runs up and pitches the ball at him 'full toss.' He swings in an exaggerated lunge but does not make contact with the ball coming at him at 50mph. Everyone boos and titters, and the taunting song starts again. He knows he has to hit the next one. His mouth is dry, his vision blurry, and his stomach in knots. This time the ball pitches close to his feet, spins and changes direction. He tries to divert his arms but he has miscalculated: it is too late! The ball smashes through the 'wickets' behind him, and he is declared OUT! The boys cheer and seem to derive malevolent pleasure from his 'outing.' "We told you, *hijras* can't play," someone yells. The sun is setting by now, and all the parents have gone home for their evening tea. The mood changes imperceptibly. Someone pushes him to the ground to see how he will react. He is ashamed, defeated. He doesn't get up. "Let's look between his legs!" they shout, starting to surround him. Hands start pulling at him, and at his clothes. He lashes out using the bat as his weapon. Someone punches him; another well-aimed kick almost knocks him out. He drops the bat, squirming to get away from the crush, and runs. He is small and lithe, and running comes to him naturally.

He keeps running for a long time until he is out of reach of those hands, of those jibes and of the reminders of his emasculation.

* * *

He is 25. He is nervous, more nervous than he has ever been before any other dance performance. They are waiting in the eaves as the music swells and the crowd offstage starts to cheer. He is unsure of the way the sheer *dupatta* is draped on his head, uneasy about tripping over the beautiful fabric that falls across his ankles, uncertain whether the bodice embedded with little mirrors and intricate embroidery will stay on! But he also feels oddly graceful with the way the anklets tinkle as he walks and the multi-colored glass bangles jingle when he moves his arms. He starts to think about his journey.

In school the boyish swagger had come easy to him once he was performing. Onstage, he had been able to step out of his body and mimic the cheesy moves he had learned from the latest boy band video that had been playing on repeat on MTV (much to the chagrin of his grandmother). He knew how to play the TV version of 'teen heartthrob'. How to actually be comfortable in his own skin while not on stage still remained a mystery to him. His masculinity had always been an "issue". Growing up he had often been described as effeminate, as a sissy. His family called him "mama's boy" – a pejorative description for what they described as his overly "sensitive" nature. Puberty had hit him late. He was smooth skinned and sans facial hair until fifteen. Even his voice had not broken, which was an excuse for his siblings to tease him mercilessly.

He didn't understand it. What did it mean to be a "man's man" anyway? And more importantly why was it so horrid to be a girl? All the Bengali religious rituals of his people focused on the worship of goddesses and yet, he was told he ought to be ashamed for being "girlish." He just knew that whatever it was that people wanted him to be, he was definitely NOT it. He was odd, ugly and could not be loved. He had wondered: since he was supposed to be a girl, would it be easier to act and dress like one? He started trying on his sister's outfits in secret. When he looked in the mirror, he saw that his slight build and soft features would make it easy to pass for a girl. He did not relate to any of the masculine characters on TV or in the Bollywood movies anyway. He wanted to feel beautiful, to be wanted, to be pampered and taken notice of. It seemed to be easy for Aishwarya Rai, the actress he idolized, to make people like and admire her. But he knew trying to dress up was wrong and that he was crazy for having such thoughts. Everyone else was right. He was sick in the head. No other boys wanted to dress up in women's clothes and dance gracefully in the hopes of attracting a man and making them fall in love with them. If anyone ever found out, he would be ostracized and teased relentlessly. He had decided to bury his unnatural understanding of the world and fit in. He carefully studied what and how he was supposed to act like, so he could escape bullying and make friends. Enter the boy bands: NSync, Backstreet Boys, 98 degrees and Westlife! Somehow, people seemed to love their fresh boyish faces, hairless bodies and not-so-traditionally-masculine mannerisms. He had studied them as if his very life depended on it: the way they walked, their dance moves, their style of clothing, their way of speaking – everything that he could pick up from them so he could stop being the social pariah.

His dance partner Munni squeals, "Errmagawhddd! It's time," bringing him back to the present. As he steps on stage and the song comes on, the nervousness leaves him. The crowd, his trepidation, the self-hate are forgotten. He starts dancing to have a good time. The song lyrics from the classic Bollywood movie soundtrack are raunchy and suggestive. "*Chholi ke peeche kye hai* (what's under your blouse baby), *Chunri ke neeche kya hai* (what's below your scarf baby)" the song's chorus queries euphemistically. It's a crowd favorite. People start to catcall, clap and sing along! In his head, he formulates a truthful answer to the questions the song poses. "*Chholi ke peeche* is my friend's padded sports-bra; *Chunri ke neeche* is a long haired wig from the thrift shop. And you know what? It's NOT a big deal, and it does NOT make me any less of a man." Offstage, breathless and sweaty from exertion he can hardly believe it. He has enticingly danced a cabaret number dressed up in a skimpy *lehanga-choli* outfit in a bar full of Desis---and lived, to tell the tale!

* * *

He is 11. The harsh steady, elongated ring of the rotary dial phone pierces the silence in the middle of the night. He wakes up and rubs his eyes, his grogginess slowly being replaced with a feeling of dread. This can't be good. Any news in the middle of the night is bad news. Long-distance calls in India are still very expensive and hence rare in their household. His grandmother says "*Oothash na*, don't pick up." As if doing that will ward off whatever evil lay in wait at the other end. He doesn't remember the next couple hours well. His sisters collapse, his mother faints, his grandmother wails loudly. They shut him into a room and ask him to go back to sleep. He eavesdrops on their conversations with his ear to the door. "Heart attack... body found... don't know when... what will happen to us... told him not to leave." Bits of sentences float in. He falls asleep sitting by the door.

The next day there is a casket and hordes of wailing relatives. No one actually tells him what has happened. His uncle takes him aside and says "You are the man of the house now. You cannot cry." His mother is hospitalized from shock. He feels uncomfortable in their tiny apartment, now being overrun by strangers. Why was he not supposed to cry? Suddenly he sees a familiar face, the neighborhood barber is there. Maybe he would talk to him and tell him stories as usual. The barber takes him out to the balcony and shaves his head in silence. And still no one tells him anything, well other than "don't cry." He hates looking at his tonsured head. He's watched this in movies; it's a Hindu ritual done after someone dies. It starts to sink in. His father is dead. And he does not know what he is supposed to do. A good-natured portly neighborhood aunty takes him aside. Her puffy eyes give her away but she says haltingly, "He is not dead, *beta*, he is just gone away for a trip." He retreats behind the safety of sarcasm and lashes out, "Well, this is a lot of crying for someone on a trip." She recoils, "What is wrong with you? You should be ashamed of yourself for behaving this way." The next day everyone piles into a car without explanation. They reach a long, grey, somber-looking building where several other people have assembled. Everyone is wearing white, except him. The paint is peeling and there is an odd metallic smell in the air. Everyone is assembled around the wooden box, which he has not looked into yet. He looks around and sees faces he knows. He is suddenly pushed into the middle of the circle. They start undressing him and he is horrified to suddenly be naked. Strong hands quell his involuntary struggles; a white *dhoti* is wrapped around his waist. A priest starts chanting grim verses in Sanskrit, a long dead language he does not understand. Another hand pours cold water on his head. He gasps and recoils. *Ganga jal*, holy water to purify his sins. "My sins? What have I done now?" he wonders. The ritual cleansing continues. He has been doused a couple of times, shivering in the morning winter cold and acutely ashamed of standing in front of a crowd in his now-transparent loincloth. He doesn't remember when he started to cry but someone gruffly reminds him "stop whimpering and follow instructions like a good boy." They open the box in the center and his mother screams and collapses again. He has not heard her like that ever before. Suddenly the priest lights a torch. The roaring flame is orange and bright amidst the grey gloom and white silhouettes in the hall. The torch is thrust in his hand without warning. He has seen this before in movies. This is the other Hindu custom. He should've known! He is horrified at what is going to happen. They start pushing him towards his father's body. He thinks that they will make him light it on fire. Will he have to burn his own father? Will he have to set fire to the hands that had held him a month ago and the face that had smiled at him as he packed his school lunch? Will he have to stand and watch another human being burn in front of him? He has been strictly forbidden from playing with matches all his life, and now he is supposed to burn a person? He hears a scream leave his mouth. He does not recognize the voice or the hysterical crying. They start pushing him towards the box in the center of the room. He is kicking, screaming and squirming to get away. He drags his feet against the cold grey floor, but the hands are strong. The torch is in his hand and he sees another man's hairy forearm clamp down on his weak wrist and bring the orange roaring down towards the box. He shuts his eyes in horror of what he is about to do. Eventually he collapses.

On the car ride home the men discuss politics and the upcoming general elections. It's as if the morning's events had not just happened. He learns an important lesson: emotions are not to be felt. They get in the way and interfere with living. Pack them away. Keep moving. Don't analyze. Don't grieve. Don't dream. Just keep moving. Just survive…

* * *

He is 28. He is folding his partner's clothes. Part of him objectively marvels at the odds and ends that accumulate in the course of a four-year relationship. The clothes are going into a bag. To be returned. He has been putting this off for weeks but it has to be done. He wishes that they could have resolved their differences. He wishes that he had not let his past affect his current relationship. He wishes he had been more patient, and less angry. More open and less pursuant of an ideal relationship that would help "complete him". But he had not yet figured out how to let the past go. Just like he hadn't figured out how to let his lover go.

They had been happy. He had loved traveling together, buying clothes and furniture together, exploring new restaurants, geekily devouring new authors, passionately arguing about indie flicks they watched and the easy intimacy when they made love.

As he folds another shirt he smells the scent he has grown accustomed to. The one he nestles up to and can fall asleep on, no matter how anxious he has been. He hurriedly wipes away tears that seem to be threatening to overwhelm him. His mother is sitting across the bed watching him. She does not seem to understand what to do with his grief *"Why are you crying? It's not like you two were married or anything,"* she says. To her the relationship had come into existence merely 8 months ago, whereas for him it had carried him through several sea changes in his life. He continues to fold the detritus from the life they had shared. *"Do it another time na, if it is making you this sad,"* she says. *"I don't even understand. Kaano? Why you have decided to give up if anyway you are wanting it so bad?"* she continues. "Did you not cry when you put away Dad's clothes after he passed away? How is this any different?" he ventures. She stiffens up and responds, "That was... different. We were... married. We... had... children." He asks her if she thought marriage and children were the only things that had held them together. She looks perplexed; no one has asked her this before. She is unaccustomed to talking about feelings, especially ones that make her vulnerable. The silence between them stretches on. He wonders if he has pushed too far. She retreats to her room, aloof and impregnable.

A while later she returns, sits down next to the open bag and starts folding up odd pairs of large socks that have escaped the washer unscathed. "Actually, I never had the courage to go through his things," she confesses after a while. "They're in a box in Mumbai. Maybe ….someday…when you come home, perhaps…" He reaches across. They hold hands. They cry, gently at first, then with large audible sobs.

She may not fully understand how same-sex love works just yet, but she understands loss. Their grief silently unites them without the need for further explanations…

* * *

He is 13. He is waiting, listening to the series of high-pitched electronic beeps and clicks. It sounds like he's decoding a transmission from outer space. There are screeches and counter-screeches varying in pitch, interspersed by static. He commiserates with the modem's distress as it attempts in vain to connect to the World Wide Web over the dial-up telephone. Computers and the internet are new to him. He is trying to check his email at a cyber-café, one of the many that are popping up at corners as jobs in 'information technology' boom in Hyderabad. A slight misspelling of *hotmail.com* redirects him to a completely different website. The pictures he stumbles upon surprise and disgust him. They certainly feature males, but he has never ever thought of males as 'hot'. It is like a car crash that he can't tear his eyes away from! He clicks through the images and does not understand the feelings that they stir up in him. He is horrified at some of the sexual acts that the men are doing to each other. He leaves….only to return. He is scared of the images, scared of what they make him feel, terrified of being found out. He can't make sense of his emotions. They frighten him. He knows he is different, but unsure how. Something is wrong with him but he doesn't know what.

"Normal" relationships have always been mysterious and unfathomable to him. Ever since he was four he remembers fantasizing that one day he would be transported to a different place. Maybe there's a world where his father is not sick, where his family is happy, where he has enough to eat, and his clothes are not hand-me-downs. A place where there isn't instability and fighting at home, and he isn't anxious most of the time. He has always known his father as several different people all rolled into one. Baba can be angry, happy, loving, raging, hallucinating, caring, paranoid, attentive, abusive, generous, violent and gentle – all in the same day! His Baba reminds him of the story of Dr. Jekyll and Mr. Hyde: a person who is kind and jovial on the outside but sporadically cruel on the inside. Baba, his protector, is unpredictable and not to be trusted. Only years later does he begin to understand and comprehend the effects of the imbalance of chemicals in his Baba's bipolar brain that explains his behavior.

Even as a teenager he cannot analyze or talk to anyone about these things. Mental illness and sexuality are both taboo topics in India. He has learned from news stories that 'deviants' in either category are not tolerated by Indian society, socially ostracized and often brutally murdered. So he escapes into books. The magical worlds of Harry Potter beckon! Escaping into an alternate universe is tempting. He does not have to remember any trauma. He does not have to analyze his frightening and repulsive feelings about sexual pictures of men. The Harry Potter books help him develop coping mechanisms. He does not understand the concept of clinical depression yet. The books explain that *dementors* are creatures that you cannot see. These creatures surround you and feed on your happiness and your soul, slowly draining you of your will to live. Those feelings of abject desolation and loneliness, those times when he cannot remember any positive or happy memories, well those are the times that he is surrounded by *Dementors*. It will be more than a decade before he hears the word compartmentalization. But he already loves the *Pensieve* from the books, an instrument you can use to watch memories only when you *want* to watch them. At other times you can simply siphon them out of your head and put them away in a glass vial for perusal at a later time.

He creates his own little vials for the memories that have a tendency to overwhelm and haunt him, for his perusal, maybe at a later time…

* * *

He is 20. He has been in the US for two years and he has become increasingly aware of his 'unnatural urges'. He understands the word gay but the portrayals of gay people he sees do not resemble him even remotely. He has to figure this out! He knew of married men in India who often had sex with other men. He *must* be one of those! He decides to lose his virginity and have sex – with a man. He cannot risk being seen by anyone so he creates a fake profile on a dating site. He has to do this fast before he loses his nerve. Within an hour online he arranges to meet with an older white man. He travels to the stranger's apartment and knocks on the door, fighting an impulse to flee. The man is even older than he had said online, and persistently persuasive. "I have to get very drunk to go through with this. There is no going back now," he thinks to himself. The man is very eager to supply him with alcohol. "Can I see your ID?" the man says as he pours a strong shot of vodka with some pineapple juice. He panics because he has used a fake name and address. Seeing him hesitate the man explains, "I just want to make sure you're over 18. You look very young." Once convinced that he won't be prosecuted for his actions the man proceeds to ply him with more drinks. "Why don't we get more comfortable?" he says lecherously, leading him to the bedroom by the hand.

Afterwards he feels ambivalent. Being touched and wanted make him feel free, beautiful and excited. But he also feels dirty and disgusted by what he has done. He is unable to look at the man. As he washes in the bathroom he scrubs his skin till it feels raw. Yet the feeling of 'unclean' lingers. He averts his eyes from his reflection in the mirror...

* * *

He is 22. He finds that the very characteristics that made him unattractive in Indian society suddenly make him immensely Desirable in popular gay culture. Being smooth-skinned and small is fetishized and fantasized! Western society seems to be obsessed with youthfulness and thereby associates youth with beauty. He learns that he is a *'twink'*, a gay slang term originating from the candy bar 'twinkies' referring to effeminate, slender, smooth-skinned guys. He is surprised that people find him attractive after years of internalized hate and discomfort over his appearance. He begins to love the attention! His brown skin is now classified beautiful and exotic. His ethnicity becomes a symbol of culture, and something to be collected by other men. He is happy! He is not going to complain about being someone's fetish. Isn't this what it feels like to be wanted? His newfound confidence helps him start to come out to a few friends and he feels comfortable being gay in Caucasian-dominated spaces.

He finds that being a twink comes with certain responsibilities. First, he has to act dumb (no conversations about stem cell research please). Second, he cannot be a high achiever. It is best if he aspires to find a job in retail or hospitality services. Third, he absolutely has to be obsessed with fashion. *"Gurrrrl, whachoo wearin tonite?"* is a very real and important existential question. Fourth, he has to be judgmental and catty; gossip and commentary, preferably negative, are essential whilst travelling in a clique of fellow-twinks. And finally, he has to always be dressed to the nines so other guys will pay for him (his self-worth being mostly determined by how much he can get other men to spend on him).

But gradually he begins to realize that once again he is pretending to be someone else just to fit in. This sense of community isn't enough…

* * *

He is 23. He has heard legends about how fabulous the Pride parade in San Francisco is. He has been saving up money for a year and can finally allow himself to experience it. He knows *one* other gay man in the entire city. A single, white male in a city of a million, this friend will be his portal to everything *gay*! He starts looking up clubs he would like to go to, markets he would like to shop at, neighborhoods he'd like to walk through, and most importantly, the themed parties he'd want to explore. There seemed to be a party of every flavor. He could pick them based on the kind of music he liked, or the kinds of guys he was attracted to, or the kinds of kink that titillated his fantasy. So many niches! Surely there would be a niche for him?

Since accepting his sexuality and finding community in queer spaces, he hadn't been able to shake off the feeling of being accepted, but still being an outsider. It had started to bother him that the first things people noticed about him were the color of his skin, and his accent. Try as he might, conversations at parties or on dates somehow returned to the loaded question, "where are you from?" He has learned to just get to the point and answer "India," since otherwise they end up in a cat and mouse game consisting of "No, but tell me where are you *realllly* from?" until that answer is reached.

On a particularly unfortunate date the month before, he had been faced with further banalities. "Oh, I *love* the Taj Mahal" and "Basmati rice is my *favorite*. Is that what you eat?" followed by, "Hot yoga is *so* good.

How often do you do it?" and, "What caste did you grow up in?" He had bitten back a sarcastic retort. "Oh really, what a coincidence! I happen to be in love with the Golden Gate Bridge, American corn, and middle-class guys who enjoy 'hot' *twerking*! We should *totally* be boyfriends!" The questions are well meaning and harmless, but they set him up as the 'other,' the one who is different in a room full of 'homegrown' lesbians and gays. He has been polite but his patience has worn out. Maybe the next time he should deadpan, "Funny you should ask, yes of course! I grew up doing yoga on the lawns of the Taj Mahal eating Basmati rice grown in its gardens."

Nothing could've prepared him for the spectacle that was gay pride in "The City." San Francisco is teeming with people on Pride weekend. There are lesbians and gays and trans* people and queers of all shapes, colors and ages! He has never before experienced such freedom. He can no longer tell who is gay and who is heterosexual, and no one seems to mind. Entire families have turned up to watch, complete with kids in strollers and grandparents in wheelchairs. This is so very different than what he had grown up with. The shame and the secrecy surrounding gays does not seem to exist here. And then suddenly amidst the gaiety, he hears the familiar beats of a *dhol*. As the parade float gets closer he realizes that the melody reminds him of home, with poetic lyrics in Urdu that mirrored his longing. On a float coming around the corner is a contingent of people who look like him. They are dancing to a Bollywood number with reckless abandon, amidst a sea of colorful fabric. There are Desi men and women marching proudly amidst the colors of the rainbow, in *sarees* and *kurtas*. He realizes that there are others like him! An *overwhelming* number of others! And by the looks of it, they are comfortable and happy being openly queer AND Desi. He is not alone! This revelation, takes his breath away. All of a sudden he realizes the piece that has been missing in *his* queer community. One of the women on the float sees him rooted to the spot, staring up at her. His elation must've shown on his face because the stranger reaches out and hands him a pamphlet. "Trikone offers a supportive, empowering & non-judgmental environment where LGBTQ South Asians and their allies can meet, make connections and proudly promote awareness and acceptance of their sexual identity," it said. When he looks back up from reading the flyer he feels an invisible hand is pulling him.

Without much thought, he jumps over the barricade separating the parade from the onlookers. He runs after the laughing, dancing group that is making its way down the main street. As he plunges into this sea of brown he feels a sense of familiarity, of belonging. He jumps up on the truck decorated with flowers, and waves at his one white friend, his portal to the city, who is quickly being swallowed up in the sea of white faces behind them…

* * *

He is 29. *He stares at the bottle labels and the names conjure up images of molecules in his head. He remembers that frightful year of organic chemistry required in his training to become a physician.* "How does this one change my brain chemistry again?" he wonders idly as he swallows it with a sense of relief. Even if current neuroscience cannot precisely explain how this little pill, held together by covalent bonds, is doing what it is does, it saves his life. One day at a time! The volume on the voice inside his head that used to tell him he isn't good enough, has been turned down. The constant anxiety, nightmares and chronic sleeplessness are being managed. He no longer spends his days wondering what is wrong with him. His "insides" match his "outsides."

Two years prior, his *Pensieve* had stopped working. He was unable, any more, to keep his memories in vials and his life in compartments. He would be raging one day and listless the next. No one understood his seething resentments and violent outbursts, not even him. No one could make sense of his depression either. They saw his promising career, his loving relationship, his financial stability and his supportive family, and declared that he *should* be happy. They said that depression was a 'western malady.' That it was an excuse lazy people made for their failures. That he was being ungrateful for all the blessings that he had. After years of silent suffering and various half-measures to cope, he had to make a decision. He could choose to face his demons and his past, or he could continue to try and live a double life. He had chosen the former. He reasoned that if he could face the stigma associated with being gay and survive, he definitely could handle facing the stigma of mental illness. He decided to *'come out,'* a second time. This time to a professional who specialized in Dialectical Behavior therapy for post-traumatic stress disorder.

He gazes absentmindedly at the contents of the medicine cabinet above his sink. A bottle of *Parachute* coconut hair oil is fighting for space beside the bottle of *Dolce & Gabana* cologne he loves. The strong smelling *Amrutanjan* camphor balm and the *neem* extract based antibacterial *Margo* soap seem to be interlopers, beside his hipster glasses from *Warby-Parker* and the styling gel from *Bumble & Bumble*. But he is at peace with being an interloper at last. After all, it gives him a perspective no one else has!

He spits out the last of the *Close-Up* cinnamon flavored toothpaste he enjoys so much and shuts the medicine cabinet. His reflection smiles at him as the thought crosses his mind "I *finally* like my life. Who would'a thought?"

5

Overthinking Desire

J. Krishnan

So, my name is Pinky, Pinky Kapoor. Yes, James Bond copied me. I grew up in a rich, white part of OTP (outside the perimeter) suburbia in Georgia. I was *that* brown kid who was mediocre at everything – and I mean *everything*. I was pretty much the definition of average ~~Jane~~ Jasminder. My high school graduation was accompanied by a blissful ignorance surrounding white privilege and hetero-normativity. Hell, I was reluctant to use the word *feminism* in the fear that my already tom-boyish habits plus using *that* word would categorize me as the bra-burning, stereotypical, butch les-, lesb-, lesbia- You know, the L word.

I ended up attending Georgia State University, located in the heart of Atlanta. I moved into the on-campus dorms with two incredible roommates. Things were already changing. I was on my own; nobody to report back to, nobody checking on my whereabouts. I felt free. On my first day of class, my then close-minded brain expected to find a replica of my high school classroom. Let me just clarify, that didn't happen. The number of African Americans with whom I'd interacted increased exponentially. In one day, it went from one to at least fifty. Mind blown. Everyone was so alive, in spirit, in music, in dance. We had a courtyard in the center of campus where Greek organizations would perform their steps and strolls.

Somewhere in the middle of my college education, I realized that I'd regret going through college without a WST 101 horror story, so I registered for a summer semester. The class looked pretty normal, no buzzed heads, no men in tutus...phew. My professor was also startlingly gorgeous, which made going to class a lot easier. I mean, who doesn't have an authority figure attraction complex these days? Teachers, bosses, coaches – everyone's fair game. The class was filled with new readings, new lenses to see the world through, and a new comfort with not having definitions for everything I felt. I was able to write, discuss, and verbalize the thoughts that were keeping me in a box, and I eventually broke them down. Not to mention when we covered white privilege, holy shit, a LOT of things began to make sense. You mean white people have an advantage... because they're white?! So that's what it's called. Mind blown. At that point, I hadn't allowed myself to be comfortable with the thought of exploring my sexuality, so the classes on hetero-normativity and hetero-patriarchy pretty much went in one ear and out the other, mostly because I didn't want to believe any of it. Straight, gay, it's all the same anyways; we all eat at the same restaurants, go to the same bars. What discrimination? Whatever.

Yeah, well that bubble exploded in my face real quick. I guess the knowledge didn't completely skip my ears. There were some inexplicable things happening. I began to intentionally think about my attraction and sexuality. Like, why I was always interested in out-benching the girls in the gym to get their attention. Or, why I had a debilitating attraction to my female boss at work. Perhaps most importantly, why was my relationship with the perfect man not so perfect after all?

In a bout of boredom, I got Netflix. Eight bucks a month for unlimited movies? Fuck yes. There were so many great documentaries and movies! Every genre you could think of: action, comedy, drama, foreign, gay and lesb…never mind that one, independent, romance…everything! Eventually it all got old, and my curiosity grew. It was much like the children's reaction to the psychological marshmallow test. The gay and lesbian movie link was there… but I was still under a social influence which told me not to click it. I didn't want to touch it, knowing it might make me realize something about myself. Something I didn't know if I was ready to handle.

Of course, I eventually clicked the damn thing. The first thing I see is this series called Lip Service. Click. Episode one ends. Mind blown. There was something very new and very strange happening in my pants… wait a minute. *The same thing that happened in the locker room!* Ohhh no. Oh balls. Is this…am I? …Do I like…? *NO. NO WAY. NO MA'AM. There's no way I like girls like that.* NOPE.

And then, I kissed a girl, and I liked it. My world was turned upside down. There was no cherry Chap Stick involved that time, though. It was more a combination of beer, menthol cigarettes, and months of un-interpretable sexual tension. Being taken control of, being pinned against the side of a car in an empty parking lot, and being kissed like tomorrow didn't exist pretty much forced me out of my internalized homophobic tendencies. Plus that was probably the hottest thing that had happened to me at that point. I mean, I'd kissed guys before, lots of guys….not like *lots*, but enough. None of those kisses ever felt anything close to this one. So many thoughts running through my head at once: 1. Ummm… *what?*

2. What the fuck is happening?! 3. Am I dreaming, because no kiss can be this good. 4. *What are you doing to my face, you goddess!!?* 5. Oh shit, that thing is happening in my pants again. Then it was over. And I wanted to do it again, and again, and again. (6. Can we do that again? k. thanks.)

Of course, I went home, and watched all of the queer movies on Netflix, and realized that maybe I should pay attention to the events in my pants. I tried things out with girls who I knew I'd never take home, and I came to the conclusion that I was gay. That I'd always been gay. It felt right. It felt true.

The process of being kind to myself and allowing for the possibility was the most difficult and most important challenge I'd ever faced. Yes, harder than that stupid, stupid physics problem that kept me from getting an A in the class with the jerk professor who I'm convinced ran a mink smuggling rink with his b…never mind, I digress. Taking a step back to recognize a feeling that was buried beneath layers of internalized homophobia, cultural expectations, social obligations and fear, was terrifying. It took time and many a conversation with my alter ego to decide to give myself the right to know.

Many random hook ups, bathrooms, bedrooms, and lines of coke later, I found myself enjoying the journey down south. I mean, who doesn't like Australia these days – the sounds, the smells, the tastes, the waterfalls, even a geyser if you're skilled enough…I mean lucky enough to stumble upon one. From then on, it was all sunshine and rainbows, and she lived happily ever after. The End.

Hah. Yeah, right. That was the beginning of a new chapter from hell in an already rocky storybook. In the meantime (between conquests… I mean consenting partners), I got involved in some activist work and began to find a reason to enjoy working. Having graduated with two absolutely useless degrees, I was an unemployed queer brown female who had a knack for writing spoken word and rap. Fuckin' great. That shit had Missy Elliot written all over it: "Pinky Kapoor is really poor. She charges a dollar just to hold the door or she'll knock you to the flo. And you're such a bore, you make me wanna snore. Snore like Al Gore, sleeping with his whore." Oh shit, that was Clinton, not Gore. My B. Regardless, I had to find a job and move out of my parents' house. After hella hustling, I got a job selling insurance and moved out. Life was good!

Oh yeah, fuck. Now I had to come out.

It would have been so much easier to say boink this and avoid questions for the rest of eternity... *not*.

I would prep myself for days leading up to an attempt to out myself: mirror talks, writing notes, rehearsing possible conversations, prepping for the worst reactions ever. Then I'd chicken out. I was more scared for my parents than I was for myself. If they never wanted to see or speak to me again, I would handle it. But what if, when people in the community found out, they started gossiping about my parents behind their backs? What if they were shunned from society all because of me? All because I didn't like men? Maybe it'd be easier for me to go back... fake it till you make it, right? But lesbehonest... I devoured pussy way too much to do that.

I went about my work life during the day, selling insurance to people who needed it, and at night, I frequented open mic nights, presenting some rap I'd written; it kept me sane. Things were easy, no problems, no questions, so I continued to avoid coming out.

And then...one fine fucking day, I got the call. The one informing me that Sushma Auntie's son, Kris, had just finished his residency at John's Hopkins and would be in town soon. FML. Now what. I went to meet Kris, with only one goal. Getting his really hot sister's number who was also so far back in the closet we might as well have been eating each other's ~~Turkish Delight~~ *Desi Mithai* in fucking Narnia.

Till date, we have been faithful to each other for five years and can't wait to get married. We have seen our ups and downs, but we haven't seen anything that would try and scare us apart! We are in love. Just like any other couple. Love is love. Love is blind. Love is equal. Love is relentless. Be free. Freely love. Love unconditionally.

6

Trans*forming Silence

Zain M.

My name is Zain and I am a settler on Unceded Coast Salish Territories. My ancestors are from Gujarat, my people speak Kuchi. My great great great grandparents and generations thereafter were raised in East Africa – specifically Kenya, Uganda and Tanzania. I identify as a Queer, Transgender, disabled, Muslim, non-binary Femme Desi guy. Nobody in my family ever talks about India. That part of myself is always lost but never found. I am the son of my mother who is the strongest woman I know. I am constantly reflecting on the stories of migration and trauma within my family as well as the process of colonialism and genocide that took place on the occupied lands where I reside, events that continue to have generational impacts. Home doesn't exist for me – when there are so many untold stories left out of my family's identity, years of generational trauma layered with shame and diasporic roots. Silence has been an ongoing theme in my family, especially around gender and sexuality.

> *"How do I begin to tell my mother I love her*
> *When her homeland is starting to die?"*

– Zain M.

I remember being as young as eight years of age when I was old enough to assert myself in my own identity. My best friend in second grade looked so much like the boy that I wanted to become. He was the only other brown boy in the class, and always invited me to play tag with him. I'd reminisce about the clothing he wore: blue sneakers with denim jeans and those simple loose baggy t-shirts. I wanted to be him. He was all jet black hair, comfortable and free. I wanted to embody that carefree kid that he simply got to absorb by virtue of being assigned male at birth.

Getting ready for Khane (*Ismaili Muslim House of Prayer*) was always such a struggle. My childhood memories of verbal arguments with my mother are echoing back as I write. The amount of yelling that occurred in my childhood because I was so deeply unhappy with what I had to wear is immeasurable. My closet was filled with dresses that had no longer fit my sister, and had been passed down to me with the expectation that I would wear them. I remember going to prayer and watching all of the boys pass by in casual denim jeans and baggy t-shirts while I had to wear stockings, heeled shoes and a frilly dress that I detested. It felt heavy to be a kid and feel so uncomfortable with my body and how certain clothes made me feel. I felt so much heartache over my body and I didn't know how to communicate this with my family.

This was only the beginning of my journey. Fast forward to the present and I am twenty four years old, living on my own for the first time and trying to find a balance between working full-time and going to school. There has been so much silence in my family about my identity and I feel like a lot of it centres around shame. I am only recently starting to come out to my immediate family, and this is a journey that involves constant navigating. One of the biggest struggles I had was coming out to my dad. I worried about how my gender didn't subscribe to his notions of masculinity and that he would never understand. I finally decided to tell him six months before having my top surgery last year. I wrote him a letter, along with a pamphlet about transition and one day when my mum was going to dinner with him I asked her to show him the letter. I think it was safest for me not to be around for the reaction. I also had a talk with a friend of mine about how he came out to his dad beforehand so I could prepare to make alternative plans, in case I needed to stay at a friend's house that night. Since then, my gender identity hasn't really been talked about. My dad has always had trouble sharing his feelings with me, so this is not new to me. I feel like he is becoming more understanding. Sometimes he sends me a text message when he reads about transgender youth in high schools doing activism; it is how he tries to connect. Though we don't have a strong emotional connection, I appreciate the small things he does in order to try to keep up with our relationship.

My relationship with my Ismaili community is one that I have struggled with a lot. I used to go to prayer at least once a week until I was about fifteen years old. I spent a lot of my early teenage years wondering why nobody around me in my community was talking about gender and sexuality. For myself, growing up as a QT* (Queer and Transgender) guy and an Ismaili Muslim with Ismaili Muslim family and ancestry is a very particular experience. How was I supposed to navigate gender in my own life when I still, to date know hardly any Ismaili Muslim transgender or queer people? I was never able to start a dialogue about queerness in my own community, which made navigating my gender identity really difficult. How was I supposed to learn more about my own gender identity when I feared that my community would isolate me for expressing it?

I stopped going to Khane and continued exploring my identity in isolation because I was depressed with my own body and I knew I needed to navigate that before navigating my Ismaili Community. Family friends, aunties, uncles and cousins would always ask me what I was up to in my life and I used to feel so much shame because my life was so different from my cousins, from my family, from Ismailis who were in my community. A majority of family I knew was going into business, engineering, law or medicine, and those were the kind of choices that had merit and value in my family and community. I would quickly make something up about wanting to do science when I was almost done with high school. The truth was, while so much family around me was so concerned about academics, I was constantly dreaming of the boy I wanted to become. I would have intense panic attacks because of my gender dysphoria and worries about my own transition. My goal in life since I was eighteen years old has been to transition – whatever that means for me – so that I can be the femme guy I have always felt like within.

I didn't really get a chance to experience what it felt like to be a kid. I grew up in a home with a lot of family violence. One time my mum, my sister and I were so close to leaving. I would cry under the covers with my mum or sister when my dad would verbally, emotionally, mentally and physically abuse my mother. My mum was so worried about money all the time, which kept us from leaving. We were almost out the door that one time, and she said she could not leave. She didn't know where we would go and she didn't have any savings. So with my dad we stayed, for years and years.

I often wonder what my life would have been like if we had been able to leave. I also really understand my mother's struggle in not being able to leave because of the need for a financial safety net and not knowing where she could access resources and a community that would support her and her two kids. I continue to struggle with depression and anxiety that stems from these experiences. I get scared when I hear really loud noises, and I get startled easily if someone I know comes up behind me. All of this resides with the family trauma I have carried with me since I was a kid and now into my adulthood.

One of the main reasons I stalled taking hormones for a few years is because of the trauma I carry from my dad. I was worried that if I started taking testosterone, I would become my dad. I didn't have a good male role model and it took many years of unlearning how shame and violence had impacted me from a young age to realize that if I needed to take hormones for my survival, I would not be like the man who hurt me, my sister and my mother. I could be my own guy and redefine what masculinity means to me and for me in my own life.

I was eighteen years old when I first heard the word transgender. A mentor in my life introduced this word to me; before that moment I had no idea what word described my gender identity. I don't necessarily like labels, but somehow I needed a word that was tangible, something I could hold onto and use for myself so that I could feel solid in who I was. When I was a teenager, I didn't really know anyone who identified this way and I didn't have anyone to talk to. I had limited internet access and to be honest, transitioning while living at home with my family was not something that was going to happen for me. I had so much shame about my gender identity and this shame is something I still carry with me. I carry years of shame. A lot of my shame is from silence – from feeling isolated and not having people in my Ismaili community who could hold me and say that being queer or transgender or non-binary is totally okay, and that our ancestors have my back.

My shame also sourced from the fact that I am not what my father defines as a "man." I strongly identify as femme, which for me means practicing assertiveness and compassion while at the same time being fierce and loving. Femme for me also means that I embody multiple gender expressions that range from wearing my fierce pink lipstick to wearing my basketball shorts. The multitude of gender expressions that I make space for in my own life is not what my dad sees as masculine, which is why our relationship often clashes. Shame is something I am constantly unpacking, and when I think about shame, I think about places in my body that hold shame and what that tension feels like. The location of shame for me in my body is in my shoulders and in my back, which makes sense because I constantly tried to protect my mum and sister, and was socialized to put their safety and needs before mine in the violent situation I was in. Being socialized as an Ismaili Muslim female, I felt so much silence around talking about my own gender and sexuality – it was viewed as shameful to even think about these things. Shame also comes from being told to be quiet and to talk politely and to never say no. It was not until very recently that I was able to communicate my boundaries and put my own needs first.

Since I came out to my mum two years ago, she has really been working toward supporting me. She has also met my chosen big sister, who is a lovely, fierce, kickass queer Desi artist, and my mom has spent time opening up to and connecting with her. I think of how chosen families in this example can form that connection with the woman who raised me, and how powerful that is. I know that if I am not around and if my mum needs something or just someone to talk to, she can feel free to call my chosen big sister and her partner. To know that my chosen family can be there for my mum when she needs support, means a lot to me. I

know for my mum, being able to read about the stories of other trans*
kids' mums has really helped her get to where she is. She really needed
that connection – to know how other mums are processing their kids'
gender identity, and supporting them. My chosen big sister got this book
for my mum and it has been such a valuable resource for her. From this
resource, my mum has been able to understand that she doesn't have to
know everything, and that it is important for her to be patient with me so
that she can listen and really hear what transition is bringing for me in my
own life.

There are definitely really hard parts about transition, too. The
hardest part for me about being transgender and Desi is not being able to
have a word in my language that describes non-binary gender identity in a
way that I would want my parents, aunties, uncles and cousins to
understand. Unlike my experience in learning about the word
"transgender" when I was eighteen and having something tangible to hold
on to, the experience with my parents is very different. There is no word
in Kuchi for my parents. Although I can speak and understand my
language, I rarely find other QT* Desis who speak the same language
because we are already such a small community as Ismaili Muslim peoples.

Family goes hand in hand with navigating my Ismaili Muslim
community – I have slowly been letting some of my cousins know how I
identify, and this has been extremely difficult. I constantly worry about
being outed by my family members to other extended family. One of my
biggest worries in letting family members know about my transgender
status is that they might put a lot of emphasis on my transition rather than
seeing me as a regular guy. One of my aunties keeps asking me how "the
transition" is going like it is this big exciting event in my life or something,
as if it is a party. I don't personally feel this way about my transition and I
don't like to talk about it with family because being open about
transitioning doesn't mean that it is a light topic that is always up for

discussion. One of my friends sent my aunt some blogs, videos and links talking about being supportive to transgender communities and I hope that will help my family.

While exploring my gender, I never once thought about my family when I made the decision to transition. Thinking about my family while making this important decision was something I could not even fathom. I was worried I would lose relationships with my parents and cousins whom I had so much love for. Two years ago, realizing I had to transition simply meant I could live a happy life. I knew that if I transitioned, a life of love and happiness was possible. It was so difficult for me to believe this and know that this could happen, before making my medical transition. I wanted to build a relationship with my body that was rooted in radical self-love, and for me this was only possible after getting top surgery and starting hormones. A year before medically transitioning, I had the most difficult year, constantly dreaming about what it would be like to be on testosterone and not being able to sleep properly because of this. I struggled through depression and waiting for time to pass until I could finally get my first hormone injection. The combination of identifying as an Ismaili Muslim, femme, non-binary, transgender and Desi guy is very complex. My mum has always said she just wants me to be happy, and I knew that for me, transitioning was part of truly embodying happiness and love in my body.

When she came to a new country, survival and happiness for my mum was about finding a job with benefits, supporting her kids, and finding laughter in everything she does. My mother is my hero, the strongest woman I have ever known for everything she has gone through, and for this I am honoured to be her son. Survival for me was about transition, and though my mum does not fully understand my transition, she is there when it matters.

She is constantly learning how to support her transgender son, she admits what she still needs to work on, and she is always there to make me laugh.

When I reflect on my transition, I think about the beautiful relationship I am starting to form with my body. I still navigate so much gender dysphoria since having top surgery and starting hormones a year ago but cultivating a relationship with my body that knows I am always listening is important to me. Radical forms of self-love for my body include having agency over my own body. This ranges from doing my own testosterone shot in the comfort of my home to really tuning into my body when I feel hungry, when I feel tired, when I feel like my chronically-in-pain body needs to rest, and letting my body know that my struggle is real, that my scars have value and that I can hear my pain. Tuning into my own body is one of the ways I feel strongly rooted in my identity. This is important because not all bodies are valued in the same way, so I choose to be loud with my body by embodying who I am in my skin. For example, I have dance parties alone in my room. This is my practice for how I feel about my body, a practice of self-care in a world in which disabled and transgender bodies are not valued.

There are moments when I do want to talk about medical transition and surgery – specifically when connecting with other QT* Desis. It is important to share this experience with our different struggles and have a space to talk about the realities of what it feels like to come out to family, to feel so much silence around expressing a multitude of genders, and to know that we are not alone – that my ancestors are present with me and that they too once navigated being Desi and transgender and queer.

Family has felt really difficult. As I am still early into my medical transition, going to family gatherings has felt hard. My name changes in those settings and so do my pronouns – hearing my birth name and the wrong pronouns makes my heart feel heavy. It feels so hard too, because I don't know how to respond to my birth name, and in many ways when I am in these settings, it feels like my transition is going backwards in that moment. When I am outside of that setting, I can see that I have come so far in my transition. For the first time in my life I have my own space with chosen family, I am able to grow and learn about my own identity in a supportive environment and be unapologetic in the agency I have over my body. When it comes to family, self-care often means saying no to gatherings or meeting up. I feel fatigued and exhausted after being present with family, so I know that if I am already fatigued before I even share space, my body needs to rest and stay in instead of going home for a visit.

One of the struggles I am also navigating with my family along with being transgender is navigating my identity as a person with chronic pain. I am less able to do certain activities and it takes a lot of energy and capacity to do things like doing dishes and folding laundry. Navigating this with my family has been really difficult; for them it means I can't work as much as other people or am not working hard enough. In communicating my pain with my chosen family, I know that I am supported in resting my body and listening to how much my body can handle. Navigating my fatigue and pain with my family is a constant process, as is navigating transitioning with them – all of this is an intersection of how my identities come together and how family impacts these processes in my life.

Spoken word and writing poetry are practices that have really helped me unpack these parts of my identity. Since as young as I can remember, I filled up journals and journals with poetry, which contain many feelings about gender, sexuality and experiences I have gone through. Writing, storytelling and sharing are such an important part of who I am. I know reading other people's stories has helped me so much too, because I don't feel as alone in my experience being a transgender non-binary guy. Spoken word literally saved my life when I was a teenager and it continues to be an outlet into my life today. I cannot imagine my life without the written and visual forms of poetry.

I often think about my ancestors and the queer and transgender Ismaili Muslims who came before me, who have been navigating all of this and fighting the fight. I reflect on how they knew I was going to be here, walking in the world and how they wanted me to be here living with them inside of me in every breath; it is my ancestors who teach me to be my true and authentic self, and I know they are with me most when I am completely myself in my body. And that is a breath of fresh air for me.

> *"this song is for my body,*
> *I wrote it for you,*
> *& all of the radical struggle*
> *that you have been through*
>
> *My hip is bearing so much pain,*
> *It feels so hard to swallow,*
> *the world feels like it's going too fast*
> *to keep up with my slow pace"*

– Zain M.

7

Deconstructing Desi

Harsimran Kaur Bagri

The institution of family, like any other social institution, is made up of roles, titles, rules, expectations and obligations, which in turn are influenced by the surrounding environment and culture. No two families are exactly alike, nor do they operate in precisely the same manner. Those bonds that are forged or broken, however, in similar cultural flames may stand to resemble one another. My aim in writing this piece is to tell my story and the story of my family in hopes that others facing similar circumstances may be able to relate to our experiences. My hope is that you will know that neither you, nor your family, are alone in your struggles.

For me, family is defined by the commitment that people make to one another based on a foundation of love and respect. Family are those who catch you when you fall, dust you off and lift you up higher than you have ever been before. The bonds of family surmount every other obligation one can commit to.

For my family, family is defined by the commitment that people make to one another based on a foundation of duty, obligation and blood relation. Family are those who catch you when you fall, dust you off and lift you up higher than you have ever been, regardless of the cost of doing so, while explaining to you exactly what you did wrong, in excruciating detail. The bonds of family surmount every other obligation one can commit to, aside from the one made to God.

Though our definitions of family vary slightly, up until the day that I was forced out of the closet as a homosexual person, my relationship with my family had very few points of tension. I strived to be an exemplary daughter and granddaughter – working for the family business, visiting my grandmother and great-grandmother twice a month, and putting the majority of my efforts into studying so that I might do justice to the sacrifices of my elders. I prayed for my family's health and wellbeing on a daily basis.

But, I was a bit odd

From the time I was young, I knew I was a weird kid. I chose to do things differently and seemed to experience things differently from my peers. I lived in a majority Punjabi Sikh community in Canada, and was a lifelong pupil at Khalsa School. As such, I grew up very much steeped in the teachings of Sikhi and Desi Punjabi culture. I knew the expectations by heart, but wasn't always so consistent in meeting them.

I recall particularly a sports day at school when I was in grade five. My homeroom class was meant to square off against another class in tug-of-war. As we were being instructed to our respective ends of this enormous rope, a murmur arose from my peers, "Boys to the front, girls to the back."

We had all heard the same lectures about equality between the sexes and the egalitarian ideology that Sikhi promoted, but somehow, in practice, our actions were not reflecting these teachings. Nor were our teachers intervening to remind us of our lessons. This division via gender however, did not sit well with me. Before I had a moment to process why, I had walked to the front of my class and picked up the rope at the closest point allowed to the center. I did not look back, no one questioned me, and we won the tug of war. In later moments I resolved that the reason I had stepped forward was because I had remembered my lessons and was only doing what I thought was right. What I was not able to solve at the time was why it seemed so much more important to me to make that statement; why did that moment seem to jar me far worse than my peers?

Looking back now, I think that I was subconsciously beginning to realize that owning and living my identity would be a challenge to the expectations of my community. It would be a challenge from which I could not, and would not, back down.

As far back as my memory reaches, this was my first experience in the double standard placed upon women in Desi culture. It was not, however, by any means, my last.

Standards

When I was nine years old, my mother divorced my father after years of physical abuse and infidelity. In a single day, my sisters and I went from being much praised students of a school trustee to social pariahs.

We would be pulled aside by elders of the *Gurdwara* to be given messages for our mother, mainly instructing her to seek our father's forgiveness and rescind the divorce filing. It was during this change in social standing that we came to realize just how relative and soluble the support of many of the people we had considered our extended, congregational family, really was. Many of the folks whom we had grown up being surrounded by, were suddenly whispering behind cupped hands, perpetuating nasty lies about our mother when they thought we weren't paying attention. We were on the receiving end of the Desi gossip wheels.

We lost most of our community that day. In that loss, we learnt many important lessons about patience, resilience, accountability, integrity, and duty. The lesson I took most to heart, however, was one of honesty.

The honest truth was that it was hell living in that household before my mom filed for divorce. Our culture would have us believe, however, that the sin greater than physical abuse is divorce. So that the social landscape would not be marred, we were literally being asked to pressure our mother into rejoining a household she considered a torturous prison.

We could not lie about the existence of that abuse, nor could we lie about the horrendous expectations of our culture.

Values

We left Canada and moved south to Washington State to start a new life. One where we would not be antagonized for living, breathing or simply being. As a single mother, our mom worked from dawn to dusk to put food on the table and to ensure that we never wanted for anything. While she was never able to stay for my volleyball games, she made sure I made it to every practice, jamboree, and meet in the appropriate gear with a lunch of *aloo parathay*, or a *mirch* filled sandwich.

It was never easy.

My middle sister, Gurkeert, and I became especially close, functioning as each other's main support system. We would hold long discussions on every subject from our favorite books and the characters therein, to dissections of our family dynamics and what things we ought to do and not do in order to keep our mom's blood pressure in check. We would talk about the society that we left behind in Canada after our parents divorced. We would discuss how our mother fretted that she had made a terrible decision moving us away from the community in which we were born. If we turned out badly, it would be all her fault. No one would ever let her live it down.

What we surmised was that it was not our responsibility as human beings to only be just or righteous or good. Our value was not found in that. Our value was found in fulfilling the functions of our roles properly. The most important of all the roles one could fulfill are, of course, the family roles. What good are you being a brilliant doctor if your mother is rotting away in a nursing home? What good are you being a sharp businesswoman if your children are all delinquents?

While I understand the logic behind this reasoning, it assumes something very dangerous. It assumes that your value as a human being is contingent upon another person's assessment of how well you accomplish a role. Having already seen the consequences of this way of thinking with our mother's divorce, and the reaction of the community upon her destruction of her supposedly perfect marriage, my sister Gurkeert and I made a commitment to never allow such thinking to dictate our decisions. We affirmed that we would build ourselves a community that would allow us to maintain one persona as much as possible. We, just as children often do, made bold claims about how we would make our world look, without really considering the work that it would take to get there. There were a few challenges that we did not see clearly at the time.

First, I had not yet come to terms with my sexuality and thus had not considered the toll that making a commitment to this course of action would take on either my family or myself. Second, we did not consider the fact that whilst we were actively trying to reject this way of thinking, our mother and our grandparents were still very much mired in its trenches, and that our behavior would be considered reflections of their values and thus paint them in negative light. Under the way of thought that they still accepted, we would be intentionally doing them a disservice by being authentically ourselves. They would be hurt, offended, disappointed and defensive in case we chose to be anything other than the people who they planned, worked and made sacrifices for us to become.

In attempting to live this lionized ideal of honesty while not fully understanding exactly what it was that I was trying to shuck, I realized many victories and validations and committed just as many mistakes, some of which I am still correcting to this day.

Not being Desi

Initially, I held everything negative about my family's experience in Canada synonymous with Sikhi and Desi culture. I looked for solace in the "kinder" Western experience and let go of lifelong convictions and practices. Instead of bearing comfort in the graces of *kirtan*, I grew resentful of those who sung it. Instead of tasting the delicious aromas of *haldi*, I would avoid going to the kitchen when my mother cooked. Instead of working for a better understanding of where I came from, I attempted to grow without roots.

I abandoned one path and opted for another without realizing that neither my idea of what I was abandoning, nor my idea of what I was pursuing, was more authentic than the other.

From time to time, I would come across a window into the past. My mom would cook only if neither of my sisters nor I were available to concoct something. Between the three of us elder daughters, this would not be often. On the occasions that she would step away from her desk, she would make her favorites, *dal makhini* and plain *roti*. No matter how I tried to stay away, I would be lured in by the scent and my taste buds would not deny their pleasure at dinner those nights. It was a sweet morsel of the past, but it was gone with the dishwater by bedtime.

I rejected everything that I could possibly stand to strip away, yet I could not erase it all.

Becoming me

When the film Bend it Like Beckham premiered, it immediately became one of my favorites. What I did not realize at the time was that I was gasping for anything that could pass as Desi but that I could still stomach only an assimilated, colonized, digestible tidbit.

It was the first time I saw the issue of homosexuality discussed in a Desi context. I identified with Jess as a rebel, as a tomboy and as being insanely awkward in women's changing rooms. She was everything that I thought I was, and while allusions to her possible homosexuality ran amok, fear not, for she wasn't anything of the sort! In the final scene, she confirms that indeed she is in love with her male coach and not Kiera Knightly. For my denial ridden subconscious, this was all the confirmation I needed. If she could be straight, then so could I! And of course, I did not want to end up having to vanish like her gay childhood friend, Tony...

For years, I bid my time. I never dated whilst under my mother's roof. I figured that I would one day fall in love with some man, in college, who would be my way out of a *rishta*. After all, I knew my family would only wish me happiness, though they might grumble a bit about how I got there; it was the most convenient approach to rejecting tradition while still maintaining my family. I was so far in the closet that I thought the biggest obstacle I might face would be falling for a man of a different race or faith.

In the interim, for the first time in my life, I entered a gay friendly environment. I began working a part time job at a kitschy little gift store downtown where the staff not only tolerated, but celebrated being queer - as more than half of them were so. As I grew to love and care about these people, I began to deconstruct my deeply ingrained ideologies of what it meant to be queer. These people were not kidding, these people were not damaged, and these people were not all white. Suddenly, all that I had repressed and written off as not being applicable to my life or my circumstances, began bubbling to the surface.

Facing denial

Within the embrace of this adopted family, I reflected on my ideas, my discomfort, and the motives behind my actions. Was I not telling Nani Ji that I didn't want a *rishta* because I was protecting her feelings, or was I afraid of the questions that would come? Was I choosing my words carefully with my mother so as not to worry her, or was I hiding my behavior for another reason?

As I started to understand the denial I had been living with, I had to face the awkward realization that although I had structured my life around becoming a person that I idolized as radically honest, I missed the mark in my bid for authenticity. I could not tell my family the truth about all the areas of my life.

Why?

Because I love them.

I never wanted to cause any member of my family grief. I wanted them all to be happy. Such perpetual happiness could not last, not if it was based, even partially, in half-truths or untold tales. Not if I hoped to continue to be in a meaningful relationship with them for the rest of my life.

Actually becoming me

For me this meant accepting that not only did I have a sex drive, but that I found persons of the same/similar gender attractive. Initially, I softened the blow with the idea that perhaps I found persons of other genders attractive as well, and that I could indeed still be fulfilled, without causing too much grief for my family. As I continued to deconstruct my identity and face the reality of my Desires, I had to acknowledge some truths for myself.

I am not heterosexual. I am not solely a westerner.

I am queer, I am Desi, and I have a lot of work to do.

By the time I came to terms with being gay, late in my college years, I had also come to realize that I needed to tell my family. If I did not, I would be perpetuating the system of thought that I had so adamantly rejected. Beyond that, I was nearing an appropriate marriageable age. With my eldest sister committed in a *rishta* and my middle sister leaving for Peace Corps, I would be up next. I could not live a farce while my family did their utmost to find me a match they thought would lead to my living a happy life.

By this time, however, I did understand and consider some of the challenges that I would be up against in coming out to the rest of the family.

The people I love

Throughout the years, I had continued to visit with my maternal grandparents. At first my mother did not wish for us to see them as they had not supported her when she had tried to exit the marriage, but eventually she gave in to her daughters' need to know their grandparents. In these visits, from my commitment to being authentic, instead of smiling and nodding along to the typical questions about grades, and promises to repeat *rehras sahib* directly after dinner, I would engage my Nani Ji and Chachi Ji (who was actually our great grandmother, but as the matriarch of our family, she was known as Chachi Ji to all) in questions about our past, about our extended family, and about the tenets of our religion in the face of our culture. I challenged them with the inconsistencies that I saw and demanded answers.

They did their best to quell my queries. At times I would leave satisfied, other times we would agree to disagree.

In the one instance that homosexuality was raised by my grandmother, based off of the knowledge that my eldest sister, Gursharn's best friend at the time was "a little funny," I felt panicked and utterly unprepared. It was earlier in my college years, when I was still battling the demons of denial. In fear of what might come out, I shut down the conversation and made an excuse to leave, leaving them puzzled and suspicious at my odd behavior.

I knew that my mother would be concerned that I had been hanging out with the wrong crowd, or had somehow become enamored with or coerced into choosing to live this way. I knew that she would not accept my simply telling her that I did not choose this reality. I would need to show her that I was the same girl she had raised from birth. I made the decision to spend the summer between my 3rd and 4th year as an undergraduate student at home – I would be there from mid-June to early September to prove myself to be the same responsible, committed and loving daughter and granddaughter, who just also happened to be gay.

My elder sisters, I told quite casually before moving home. I trusted them. They had been through the same experiences that I had and knew that I would not have come to this conclusion lightly. They supported me and responded with a resounding and quite telling, "Don't tell mom."

But, I had to. So I moved forward. I packed, and prepped and planned as well as I could, but nothing could truly prepare me for what I found waiting for me at home.

The plot thickens

Gursharn and I had never been extremely close and she had not been a part of the commitment that Gurkeert and I had made. I observed that she had developed a sort of defense mechanism based loosely on maintaining appearances and upholding that way of thinking that Gurkeert and I sought to reject. It appeared that this defense mechanism was activated if she were ever criticized in any way. Her reaction would be to draw attention away from herself by pointing out the errors and misdeeds of others around her.

In the months before I was set to return home for the summer, she was embroiled in a scandal with her fiancé by arrangement. She was being pressured to break off the engagement and make another match, but had fallen in love with her fiancé and was thus resisting our mother's directive. Suddenly, the focus moved from her situation to a different "problem" when she informed my mother that I was gay.

Mom, I love you

The existence of a Punjabi, Sikh, queer woman is one of the most contradictory and blasphemous ideas that she may have ever had to face. That the Punjabi, Sikh, queer woman could be the daughter of her household only served to make her even more incredulous. Incredulous that homosexuality could intrude into her gene pool, and furious at the thought that any child of hers could choose to entertain the possibility that they might take part in such a horrendously unnatural and dirty lifestyle.

She would question the environments and the influences that she had allowed her child to access. Every parenting decision would be under scrutiny. The worth of every sacrifice made on behalf of that child would be reviewed. She would then be ashamed that she could produce such a contradictory, unruly and unnatural offspring. The once shining example of daughterhood, of Sikhi, of a life's work well done, would become one of the family's greatest shames, and worst kept secrets.

This is the path that my mother traveled.

Upon learning that my mother was aware of my orientation, I approached the subject with her as I tidied her room. I asked her if we could talk about the fact that I am gay. Following a sharp intake of breath, as though she had been stung by a bee, she abruptly replied "*neyhee.*" She then burst into tears. I reached my hand out to comfort her, out of reflex. She told me to not to touch her with my gay hands. I turned on my heel and left the room.

Bonds

Suffice it to say, I did not go to my grandparents with the news that cold, cold, ninety eight degree summer. My mother and I spent the rest of that frigid summer and the following year, not talking about *it* except for the occasional emotional outburst. I would explain that this was not a choice. I would explain why I really would not choose this orientation, if I had the opportunity to choose. I would express that I knew the pain I was causing her, and begged her to believe that I would not choose to do that to her, had I another choice.

Nothing prevailed.

No explanation, time, tears, yelling matches, somber embraces, joking conversations, laughter, excitement at my graduation and the beginning of my career could change the fact that she wanted me to be heterosexual. Nothing could change the sad faraway look in her eyes when she thought I wasn't looking. As much as I could not bear to see the disappointment and rejection, I committed myself to continue to be a part of my mother's life and have her be a part of mine.

Part of the determination to stay is that I am not content to give up my mother, just as I am not content to live a lie. I understood that in order to even have access to the opportunities that I have been able to take advantage of, my mother, her mother before her, and her mother before her had all made immense sacrifices. I would not be able to stand on par with my elders nor look them in the eye if I were to settle for less than what I think is right.

It is not right for me to live a lie.

It is not right for me to give up my family.*

I cannot say that I have always been calm. I cannot say that I have always been reasonable. And I cannot say that I have never spoken a hurtful word to my mother.

I can say that I have never stopped talking. Just as my mother never has.

* Not everyone in one's blood family, however, is deserving of the title of 'family.' I do not confuse the value of shared blood to be higher than the value of action, commitment and loyalty.

Never stop

In the good times and in the bad times, I have never failed to return my mother's phone calls. I have faced every question that my mother has asked me. I have sat through her tears and her demands. I have put forth every effort in my arsenal to be in a healthy and good relationship with my mother. Just as she has.

If it were not for her cooperation, if it were not for her love, if it were not for her willingness to engage in conversation, my lofty goal would be nothing but smoke.

A year and a half out from that frigid summer, our conversations are morphing. We are not awkward around the subject of marriage, and my mother no longer brings up the deepest wish of her heart – my never-to-be *rishta*. We joke, and chat, and cook good food together. We sit and strategize for her businesses and for my future endeavours, together.

I still visit my grandparents regularly, and along with still listening to the reminders to do my *paath*, I fix their computer settings and move their furniture around to how they want it. We hold long discussions about the parts of our heritage lost to colonial rule; I learn the translations for my *Punjablish*, I learn how to best make *missey parathey*, and I learn grace.

I learn grace as I see my grandparents stop mentioning *rishtas*, but never stop telling me they love me. While they cannot completely hide their sadness, they do not hide their joy, their pride, or, their love.

Every day is work, but every day we take another step forward into our new normalcy. These are not traditional waters we are treading. In order to keep our head above the waves, we are developing a new stroke.

And for now, this is enough.

8

Contradictions and Invitations

Kurangu Paiyan

My mother, my father, and I walked in to the McDonald's. It was mostly empty, which wasn't surprising given that it was 11am on a Thursday. The person at the cash register watched us expectantly, but we walked past the line to a table in the back of the room and sat down. The chair swiveled slightly as I sat down. I fought back tears and the urge to vomit. My mother looked at me sharply and said, "We need to hear the entire story. Tell us every single thing that happened."

"What do you mean?" I stammered.

I knew what she meant. The previous night, I had decided to come out to my parents.

It had been a surprisingly sudden decision. I had spent two years wondering what that moment would feel like. I had intended to wait for at least another two years. I told myself that it would be significantly easier for me to prepare for the worst if I was financially independent. I played out various outcomes in my head as I imagined their rejection, cried real tears about the disappointment I imagined they would feel. You'd think after all that, I would have had some sort of plan.

Instead, I returned home for the summer before finishing college, experienced intense anxiety around my (gender)queerness, and somehow managed to convince myself that I'd feel better if I finally told them. I decided to write them a letter.

It felt unwieldy from the start – the concepts I typically used to describe my sexuality were all built on words I learned in college, words to which my parents would never have had access. Queer / trans / genderqueer / fluidity / colonization / binary all seemed like terrible places to start when I had never even talked to my parents about heterosexuality. I wanted to be completely honest, yet it didn't feel effective to use words that they hadn't ever heard of, to describe something I so desperately wanted them to understand. I had heard my mother use the words 'lesbian' and 'gay' before, spitting them out under her breath as if they were curse words that she didn't want us to hear. I figured those were my two options. I didn't want to use the word lesbian, because I'm not a woman. For simplicity's sake, I decided to use the word 'gay' and tell them I was only attracted to women and not men. And that was where the contradictions began. Because that's not exactly true either; I've never identified as gay, I have been attracted to men, and I certainly don't believe attraction is that static or gender that simple.

By the time I had reconfigured my identities in a way that felt more understandable to me, any description I could provide felt far removed from all the thought, emotion and complexity that I had experienced. The oversimplified, one-page letter is the best I could do.

Contradictions and Invitations

I remember that night very clearly. It was July 3rd, and fireworks were already being lit in anticipation of the 4th. Every time the sounds of an exploding cracker filled the air, I couldn't help but notice the difference in the celebration of American 'freedom' and my own attempt at navigating my queerness and brownness in this country. My parents read the letter, again and again. For all my worries and fears that they had already guessed or known in some way, they seemed to honestly have no idea what to say. The shock of reading those words and hearing me repeat them meant that their reaction that night was the mildest and most subdued of all the reactions they had in the future. They told me that I had always been the type of person to take on the worries and difficulties of others. That was true – as a kid, whenever someone else was being punished, I was always the first to cry. They told me that this was definitely a result of my spending time with gay people, that I had picked this up as my struggle when it really wasn't mine at all. My father walked out of the room. My mother even went as far as thanking me for being honest with them. I went to sleep with a strange feeling in my stomach. I had expected an explosion. I expected them to tell me that they couldn't accept it, that I would no longer be a part of the family. I expected their reaction to my queerness to be extreme. I didn't realize that in order for them to have those reactions to my queerness, they would have had to accept the fact that I was queer to begin with. For two years, I had attempted to mentally prepare myself to deal with a reaction that I didn't get. Was it really just not as bad as I had expected it to be?

The next morning, our conversation in McDonald's answered that question with a definitive 'no.' My parents spent the next few hours demanding to hear the details of my experience with my sexuality. They wanted the full story, not what was encapsulated in a one page letter. I felt incredibly uncomfortable answering any of their questions, because this was the first time we had ever talked about sexuality in my family. I didn't even get the sex talk – I just read Chapter 46 of my biology textbook, 'Animal Reproduction.' Responding to questions about who I had been attracted to and why I felt like I was attracted to women made me feel anxious, because there was no way that I could both acknowledge my sexuality and have them understand. If I were to tell them that I had sexual or romantic interactions with women, it would violate all the rules that had been set for me since childhood. I had always been told not to be attracted to anyone and not to pursue a romantic relationship with anyone. Having this conversation with them was taboo for reasons far beyond my queerness. As someone who played the role of a daughter, of a woman, I was not allowed to have sexuality at all.

As the conversation continued, I began to have the sinking feeling that I was digging myself into a deeper and deeper hole. My mother at one point stopped me and announced that she had spent most of the night doing internet research. She slowly told me that she had been looking for scientific articles so that I wouldn't think she was biased. During her search, she had apparently found some sort of article that said that people who had OCD sometimes questioned whether or not they were gay. She was convinced that I had OCD. I was thrown off course. Of all the responses I had anticipated, I hadn't seen this one coming. I stammered as I said that although there was a lot of stigma around mental health and OCD, I didn't think that was what was going on here. Her eyes lit up as she said, "That's exactly what the article said you would say." I stared at her blankly, not sure how to go about explaining to her the gap in her reasoning. I slowly began to realize that when my parents believed so deeply that being queer was wrong, the only way they could be able to reconcile their perception of me as their loving daughter and their newly gained knowledge of my queerness was to deny my queerness altogether.

As the day went on, the hypotheses as to why I might be 'confused' became more and more wild. I found myself having a hard time explaining that no, it wasn't that I had OCD, it wasn't that I spent time with deviant friends, it wasn't that I went to certain events, it was just that I was queer. In their minds, queerness was a thing that happened to me, not a state of being. I found myself repeating liberal gay sayings that I previously mocked. "Some people are just born like this, it's just like how you and Appa love each other, but with two people of the same gender." Just by the second day of my coming out experience, it was becoming obvious that I couldn't have this be about honesty and authenticity, as I had fantasized before. That would have been impossible, given the amount of personal work it would have taken my parents to even come to an understanding and acceptance of me being open about having any kind of sexuality.

That day marked the beginning of a painful blur of days strung together, becoming months, of feeling trapped between identities and understandings. Parts of it return in vivid memory – my mother telling me this queerness was repulsive, yelling at me in tears, asking how I could have gotten myself involved in this filth? My protests became softer over time, until they faded into silence. Whereas I once had ambitions of being firm and clear in my statement of my sexuality, I now could only hope that one day I would last an entire conversation with my parents without sobbing uncontrollably. Their demands were relentless. They were determined to get me back on the right track. They told me that I was forbidden from talking to queer people, that I shouldn't think queer thoughts or view queer content online. They began to scrutinize my personal life with an intensity that I hadn't experienced before. Thanks to the hyper-visibility that social media lends us, they started to try to find out which of my friends I had mentioned before were queer. It was incredibly stressful to know that my relationship with them was being impacted by what my friends were posting online. They found out that many of the people I had been working with were queer and pressured me to end working on those projects. I felt helpless. Disobeying their demands generally meant more fights, more tears, more anxiety. I felt trapped by the situation and felt ashamed that I couldn't 'stand up to my parents' as my white queer friends so easily had.

The problem was, I'm not even sure that I wanted to stand up to my parents in the way that I felt like I was supposed to. Standing up to them usually meant walking away from them. I didn't want to walk away from my family. Was having them acknowledge my queerness really worth not having them be a part of my life? Was it really that simple? That I could yell, shout and scream my so-called 'truth,' and have that mean more to me than their absence from my life? I knew I wasn't ever going to receive their acceptance. No amount of explaining on my part would change that. And to be fair, I was never going to come around to their perspective. They expected me to be heterosexual, and I expected them to accept me. Both were equally unrealistic expectations. My only hope was that in the absence of acceptance, we would still find room to love each other. But what does that even look like? What does love without acceptance look like? What does it mean to want someone to be a part of your life and still have a fundamental disagreement with how they treat you?

The more I thought about these questions, the more I questioned the stories that I had been told about queerness. I turned to a friend of mine, who had been a spiritual mentor of sorts. She was a straight South Asian woman, who knew very little about queerness, but treated me with love and kindness. I would call her at odd hours, in tears about a recent fight with my family. She would leave whatever situation she was in to listen and gently convey her loving advice over the phone. During one particularly distraught phone call, she said, *"Your mother is doing to you exactly what was done to her."* Finally, I had words for the frustrating nature of the fights I had with my family. The convenient queer narrative portraying 'homophobes' as villains, was inadequate and also simply untrue. My mother might not have experienced the control of her sexuality in the context of queerness, but she had certainly experienced it under the broader context of gender and being a South Asian woman. She was put in the position of controlling my gender, because that too, was expected of her. If I truly wanted a world in which I, as a queer nonbinary person of color, wanted to have more ownership over my gender and sexuality, it meant that I would want the same for my mother.

Some of that was easier said than practiced, though. The emotional distance between my family and I continued to grow. I found it really difficult to act with compassion and love when I felt so hurt.

In the weeks that followed, I tried to practice compassion during conversations with my family. Attempting to be there for my mother while also acknowledging my pain proved really difficult. I began to internally celebrate the times we had conversations that did not involve my queerness. These conversations gave us opportunities to maintain our relationship outside intense arguments. I accompanied them to *satsangs* and prayer groups that they were committed to. I tried to be gentler and less accusatory with my words. Most times, our conversations would still end with me in tears, but I was able to understand their views as part of a larger systemic problem rather than outright condemning them.

My life changed significantly when I began to realize that there was an active group of radical South Asians that usually met close to where I worked. I walked in late to the first meeting, looking at all the brown faces around me in anticipation. As the meeting continued, I heard them talk about food justice, black and brown solidarity, and queerness, sometimes all in one breath. I was so surprised. For the first time, I was able to bring my whole self into a space. I could be around a group of twenty or so Desi folks and trust that everyone in the room was committed to politics that included fighting for queer and trans Desis. I left the meeting feeling like, for the first time, I had met a group of people that I could consider community.

I continued to attend events, form friendships, and very quickly began to think of the group as chosen family. My evenings began to slowly fill with radical Desi dinners, art events, talks, and gatherings. Although the fights with my family were still heartbreaking, they no longer seemed as drastically consequential. I had a connection with my culture, with my community that could support me. I had something to fall back upon. There were people around me who understood. My family was aware of the fact that I was spending time with more South Asian people, but this community seemed so vastly different than my family that I couldn't bring myself to connect the two. I continued making up excuses and stories about my whereabouts, until I found out about an event on caste. I knew that my family benefited immensely from caste privilege. I went to the event, unsure of what to expect. Two incredible Dalit women activists presented about the oppression and sexual violence that Dalit women experience on a regular basis. Their words were immensely powerful and for the first time, I began to understand what a monstrosity the caste system was. I saw that my family, and all our ancestors, benefited from the violence that the caste system perpetuates. When I got back home that night, it occurred to me to lie, once again, about where I had been. The few conversations I had about caste with my family prior to that night had been very upsetting. It felt like caste would become yet another argument in our relationship. When my parents asked me about my night, I was shocked to hear myself describe the event and the two activists that I had met. I was even more shocked to hear myself ask them to join me at a repeat of the same event, which was going to be held the next day. My father didn't respond, and my mother barely nodded. I spent the next morning emailing and texting them to convince them to come. In one of the first honest statements I had made to them in months, I told them that it would mean the world to me if they attended the event. As the start time approached, I felt like I was going to vomit. I felt like I was coming out to them all over again. This was probably the first time they would begin to understand my political identity. I breathed a sigh of relief as I saw my parents walk through the doors of the room. They took their seats next to me as the presentation began. As the activists began to describe the violence that Dalit women faced, it occurred to me that this was also the first time my parents had ever been part of a conversation on patriarchy and rape in India. It was probably a lot to take in. As the presentation drew to a close my father walked quickly out of the room, clearly uncomfortable. My mother, however, walked with me to the front of the room to meet one of the activists and tell her how moved she was. That night, I lay in bed realizing that I felt closer to my parents than I had in years. The act of inviting them into a part of my life, rather than pushing them away, was refreshing.

My family has not progressed in their understanding or acceptance of queerness. But I still hope that we can build upon the relationship we have outside my queerness. I hope that I can continue to have the strength to invite them into parts of my life and I hope they will do the same in return.

9

Resilience in the Hearts of Artists and Communities

Jotika Chaudhry

My Mother

I want to talk about my mother,

the woman who held me inside her body

the woman who created me

Protected me from this cruel world as long as she could

My mother is a warrior. Everyday.

fighting wholeheartedly, unapologetically

unwavering, silent, strength.

Enduring all the harshness the world continues to throw at her

Living with the pain she holds in her heart

My mother's hands are tough. Cast Iron strong.

From years of use/work/class struggle. survival
Once in a while she laughs hard and from her gut
These are the moments she is able to let go
Moments when life isn't so hard and we laugh together
Mamma mamma please don't cry.
Mamma mamma dry those eyes.

Mothers Who Are Warriors Raise Warriors

My relationship with my mom is complex. We used to scream so loudly at each other; bodies drenched in pain, hurt overflowing. We never knew how to say the right words. She is a survivor and I learned my warrior ways from her. She is a brown, immigrant woman who doesn't have a lot of job options because we live in a place that prioritizes higher education and degrees represented by pieces of paper. Her lived struggle and survival don't seem to be of much worth in this capitalist, colonial society. We grew up poor and lived in British Columbia Housing, which is the subsidized housing in our area. Mom worked so hard to put food in the fridge for us. She would always say to me, "Just get an education, so you can stand on your own two feet." These words rang in my mind because this was, and still is, her hope for me. She knows that having that piece of paper will afford me opportunities she has never had access to.

I am almost done with my Bachelors degree in Social Work, which I have struggled to get through. Academia doesn't know how to make space for poor, brown, queer artists. It is not structured to fit my slow, questioning, heartfelt pace. My university experience is breaking my spirit; I feels like it's taking all the attributes that make me beautiful, a survivor, inspiring and strong, and it's telling me I don't matter and I'm not important. It is invalidating those places where I hold insider

114

knowledge and intelligence and fucking heart strength. It's so expensive. It's unaffordable. But I'm doing it. For my mom and for myself. So that I can stand on my own two feet.

In my early 20s when I started being really honest with my mom about what I was doing in my life, I would tell her that I was going to the pride parade, and that I was the Queer Collective Liaison at my college, or that I'd be at events centered around LGBT*Q experiences. I felt comfortable telling about these parts of my life. I introduced her to a few of my girlfriends; I told her they were my friends or she assumed that is who they were. Five years ago, we were standing in the kitchen as I was getting ready to go to school and she asked me, "Are you a lesbian?" I think she asked me this after talking to one of my Aunties and putting these different pieces of my life together. But this word didn't fit for me. It doesn't embody my being, my queerness. It feels rigid and it is also from a movement that doesn't feel like mine. Speechless at mom's forwardness, I just looked at her and nodded my head. It seemed like it wasn't that big of a deal for her; she asked me a few questions. She drove me to school and the whole time I was in shock and wasn't sure what she was asking me and felt in disbelief that she seemed fairly calm about the whole thing.

At the time my sister was in the hospital and was recovering from surgery. As mom was driving she said, "Oh ok, it doesn't matter; we have bigger things to worry about than that." I had been terrified to tell her; I made up stories in my head about how she would react. I had felt so certain that she would not understand or be able to accept who I am. Her response shattered the fear I had created within myself.

When I was a "baby gay" and just coming out in my early 20's, I felt the shame and silence that existed within my family's untold, unspoken stories. I understood that there were things we just didn't talk about; we didn't talk about the things that hurt us, or trauma that we caused one another. I now realize that this silence just gets held in our bodies. Ancestral stories no one talks about or even knows. I realize that my queer sexuality is okay and can exist, as long as I don't talk about it with my extended family. Whispers of, "Do they know about you?" "Don't say anything about...you know," tell me where I need to keep the silence with my family.

My queer community and my family existed for years within separate containers. At home, a part of my life existed that we didn't necessarily talk about. This is slowly starting to shift, like when I bring my partner to a Diwali celebration at my Bhabhi's house, where only a select few know who she actually is. It still hurts a lot not to be able to share my life experiences, my stories, my love with some of my family. Even when my partner is around, it is as though our relationship is the elephant in the room that no one is talking about. At least not to my face. I worry about people talking about my mom and her feelings getting hurt. I know she worries about people talking behind her back and shaming her for having a queer daughter, a daughter who is anything other than heterosexual. When I am with certain family members, queerness just isn't something we talk about; it isn't something I necessarily feel safe about bringing up.

Diaspora lives in my bones, heart and in untold stories

My homeland, the land I am indigenous to is in Northern India: U.P., Uttar Pradesh. I don't know if any of my family is still there. This fact is heartbreaking to me. I have never been to my homeland; never put my feet in the Indian Ocean or touched the earth that my par-par Aji and par-par Nani (my great-great grandmothers) were from and grew up in. I've yet to touch the soil that my ancestors were born on and worked in. My family's stories center around being uprooted from their homes. My ancestors were indentured labourers brought to work on sugar cane plantations. The English used brown people to do that grueling work – the sweat and hard labour. I come from generations of hard workers and farmers, who did back-breaking work to earn more for their family. I think about the stories that have got lost in travel. Those whose tears no one talks about and can't remember.

My mom is Catholic and she attended a school in Fiji, run by nuns. After coming to Canada, that's the religion she went back to; the religion that gives her peace and solace. I am a baptised Catholic too, but this religion has never felt like home to me. I've gone through with the motions of being Catholic because that is what I was expected to do, but now I've stopped going to church and stopped praying to Jesus and Mary. My family are mostly Hindu on both sides, and my religious lineage is Hinduism. My mom is the youngest of fourteen siblings, and most of them, as well as my Jijis and Jijas, Mamas and Bhabhis, are Hindu. I feel I was born a Hindu and it is in my blood. I went to *Pooja* with my mom but I was so little I can't really remember a lot of it. I feel I have lost a huge part of myself being raised Catholic; I didn't get a chance to learn Hindu songs, prayers, or about our rituals and celebrations. This absence aches in my heart. I feel the loss. I come from generations of Hindus and religion is how I connect with my family, my ancestors and my past. It is the vehicle through which we celebrate weddings and funerals for our loved ones and with our loved ones.

I know there is a lot of patriarchy ingrained in the teachings of Hindu scriptures and rituals. Teachings that talk about women being inferior to men and/or about very binary, rigid gender roles. As I learn, I can sift through those parts of Hinduism that don't feel right to me. But I would have loved to have been given the opportunity to learn when I was growing up. I would have loved the choice to celebrate with my extended family, practice rituals and learn the meanings behind it all.

I can't communicate in my mother tongue. I can't say what I am feeling, or tell a story. I am unable to complete a full sentence without English, my colonized tongue taking up space and saying the words from my mother tongue inaccurately. I am re-learning the words, the tones, the beauty of the way the language moves and feels in my mouth. Learning from the women: Ama, Aji, Nani, Par Aji, Par Nani. From their stories – from the precious wisdom in the stories and in old photographs. I don't need to hear from other people, especially non-Indian people, how colourful, bright, beautiful, intricate, amazing they think my culture is. Especially if it is something they learned from a textbook. I've lost it and I don't need to hear it. I will discover it for myself.

My parents immigrated from Fiji over thirty five years ago and were displaced here, on Coast Salish Land. I used to say I was Fijian. I am not Fijian; the Native Fijians are the Fijians. Nor do I think this is my land. We just settled here on Coast Salish Land. I am Indian. Generations of diaspora later, I am still figuring out what that means for me when there is so much disconnect. I am a child of diaspora; I feel like parts of me are scattered in different places in the world. Years of displacement sit heavily within me. The broken Hindi echoes the pieces of my mother tongue that is in fragments in different oceans, buried in scattered soil. Part of figuring out my history is trying to pick up those pieces. It's not easy and no one tells you how to do it. It comes from within, it comes from trying to hear my ancestors' words, hoping they would want me to be happy. It means figuring out what happiness, inspiration and belonging mean to me. Listening to the strong women, my queer ancestors, all the warriors.

Radical unapologetic coloured queer love

The love that Lydia, my partner, and I have queer, coloured, and body affirming, confuses mainstream society, people outside of our queer bubble. When we walk the streets, people are not used to seeing our brown and yellow skin together, an interracial queer couple, our bodies fat, curvy and round together. Every day we are inundated with heterosexual images of thin, hairless, white people holding hands, Desiring one another and laughing on TV, the internet, ads and movies.

In the context of these images Lydia and I are not 'supposed' to love each other or Desire one another or celebrate love together. I feel it when people stare at us on the skytrain or do double takes when we are walking down the street with our hands intertwined. I experience people whispering, making comments overtly, covertly. Our resistance to these messages lies in showing public displays of affection, holding hands, wrapping our arms around each other and flirting. We are making space for our narratives, taking up and reclaiming space. We help create visibility, creating a world in which we can Desire one another. We celebrate our queer, coloured, body loving, body positive, fat, dyke love. We celebrate by choosing to be together, by loving one another.

Pieces of my resistance exist and come from the ways I love her. The touching of our bodies is an act of acceptance and transforming the status quo; it's freeing. Healing comes from every touch. Learning how to communicate in healthy ways heals past trauma and pain.

Growing up in my home, there was a lot of yelling. We threw hurt at each other. I was so angry. Growing up in violence means that the physical and emotional pain sticks with you; compounded by years of intergenerational wounds. Socialized as a brown woman, I was taught, as a lot of our women are taught, to suck it up, to not take up a lot of space and to care for everyone else. In my home we didn't talk about our feelings or say sorry when we hurt each other. Violence created fear inside my brown body which kept me from getting close to people in an intimate way. This fear created and fed anxiety, self-doubt, low self-esteem. This body is fearful at times when there is nothing to be scared of; when confronted with conflict at work or in social settings, I jump into flight response and just want to escape.

When one gets hit as a kid and is highly sensitive, as I am, it affects one deeply. That fear and anxiety get trapped inside. I cried all the time and no one understood why. I didn't have the knowledge or language to explain. My pain was deep-rooted, compounded by emotional stress and the inability to process these experiences. With every kiss, with every time Lydia and I say I love you – *"Hum Aap Ko Pyaar Kartha"* – I feel less fear in my body. It hurts a little less. It has taken me years of work though; years of unlearning, conversations, counselling, and I'm still working on it. I realize now that my tears are not something to feel shame around. Self-love has been a journey. Healing is a process. Building relationships based on trust and respect is breaking the cycle of violence; learning about what I need and what I deserve is creating new patterns.

I grew up not Desiring my own body, not appreciating the beauty that is my brown body. I always wanted to change something – be smaller, less hairy, lighter. My heart and the hurt I carry loosen up when Lydia touches me, when she holds me. Healing comes from this kind of honest, compassionate, heart-centered love. Where even though self-love is hard, I let someone else in and let them show me that I deserve to be loved. I let someone care for me in the ways I was never cared for. I give myself that compassion radically and shamelessly, and over time I've started to hurt less. It took Lydia and my chosen family saying: I love you, you are enough, you work so hard and you are beautiful, for me to start believing that these things are true about me. Then I started saying them to myself, and I still work at believing these words about myself.

Lydia and I are honest in those tough kind of ways; we call each other out on things we need to work harder at. We hold and make space for each other to grow and learn. We hold each other's painful, broken parts, and we love fearlessly, courageously. We are accountable to one another and to the communities that we build, and when we fuck up, because we do fuck up, we talk about it. Lydia's arms are a safe and warm place where my anxiety ceases to exist for moments at a time.

Covering up/uncovering

You keep saying you keep saying everything is all ok

Babies know. Felt senses in utero before they are born. Waves of attunement flow through their small bodies.

It's not about remembering that fear; I still feel it. The body knows.

That lump in throat. Pulsating. Tingling in stomach. Ache. Strain. Power over.

The only way to free it is to let it flow.

Tears rolling down my brown cheeks. Scream. Pulse. Breathe. Release.

The only way to free it is to walk with it. When I wasn't allowed words, when they were unsafe.

She says memories are like melodies. Rooted inside. Ancestors. Alive within. Their stories in my blood.

Home. Fiji. Home. India.

Forced migration. Displacement. Indentured labourers. A need for survival. More hope for me. Years of struggle. Generations of strength. Stories too far to feel and too heavy to hold. Journeys on boats. Ancestral freedom songs drowned with my mother tongue.

No words to say No. Lost in the Indian Ocean.

I hold, fear, dance though, towards pain. This body hurts. Mera Dei Egdum Pirawe.

Remembering. Uncovering. You told me your truths later when I was somewhat old enough to understand. My empathy was louder than his anger.

I weep for you. My infant self remembers your tears.

I am holding you now. Me apanē pakaṛa hūm

We can walk together. Through Fear.

Fragmented.

He broke my heart too

Words are safer now. I'll sing to your heart. Maiṁ apanē dila kō gānā gātī

You keep saying you keep saying everything is all ok,

Everything is all ok.

*This is a song poem I wrote this past year about the pain of displacement paralleled with the pain of being a survivor and witness of abuse.

Survival lives in the hearts of artists and resilience in communities

I am an artist; it took me a long time to identify with that word and to feel good enough to claim it. I have always painted, collaged and wrote for as long as I can remember. I have pages and pages of truth telling in journals that I have kept since I was twelve. I was always singing or listening to music or making music of some kind. Art, for me, is healing. It is a space where I share my struggle and stories with people. It is a medium I use to share my vulnerable truths. Creating art is where I hold power in my life, where I make the decisions and where I take up space. All I ever wanted to do was write and make art and put colours on something, on anything. To make life brighter, safer, more bearable, more beautiful. Easier to stand in. Anything to help me feel more alive and less alone. I've made art my whole life, before I ever knew why; I made art to get my pain outside of my body, to help understand my feelings and to have an outlet for what I was experiencing. These forms of creation, I now realize, were coping mechanisms that kept me alive. I make pieces of art now that I wish I had when I was growing up. They hold messages of hope and support. I create song-poems about diaspora, disconnection, trauma, survival, self-love and healing, to name a few. The visual art that I create now is for myself and for people in my communities, other

QT*IPOC (Queer, Trans*, Indigenous and People of Colour). I create paintings on wood and canvas mixed with messages of love, glitter, paint and various other materials. I aim to create pieces that help uplift myself and others and to acknowledge our struggle as well as our resilience and survival.

Over the past few years I have met some amazing QT*IPOC, and have started organizing community events with them. We have spent hours in coffee shops and on living room floors, grant writing, talking and brainstorming about how to hold events that center our voices and experiences, and are created through a lens that transforms oppression. Together we have created events which center artists who are passionate about social justice and which showcase QT*IPOC singers, poets, dancers, visual/mixed media artists, musicians, comedians and many more. We have worked hard to create spaces where we feel safe and can witness connection and love within our shared struggles of diaspora, migrations, decolonization, trauma, healing, remembering, relearning and disconnection. So many of us are disconnected and displaced from our homelands, and that is a beautifully painful truth to share with someone. We honour each other and support one another. Together we aim to bring QT*IPOC together, break isolation and build supportive networks of community, spaces to share our art, talent and stories, and to create meaningful relationships. This past year I helped organize a Queer and Trans* South Asian performance night at a local café. It was a night of storytelling, laughter, tears, connections, struggle, and reconnection as well. It was one of the most memorable nights of my life. I sang for the first time in Hindi in public and burst into tears. I sang "Jab Koi Baat Bigad Jaye" and dedicated it to my sweetheart Lydia. There was a predominantly South Asian audience and they held me up, and as a community we created a space where I felt safe to just cry and sing on stage. I sang the whole song with my voice cracking and it was beautiful.

Through organizing and being in the QT*IPOC community I have met some amazing friends whom I call my chosen family. I connect with them in our shared struggles, resilience and passion for social justice, and art as a tool for healing. We are all artists and healers in many different ways. We take care of each other in ways our biological families maybe never knew how. My chosen family means the world to me and they have all helped keep me alive. I learn so much from all of them; they inspire me and we remind each other why we deserve to be happy, that we are powerful and capable and beautiful people. Meeting and connecting with these folks has been life changing.

Right now my life is about trying to reconnect with my definition of what being Indian means. Some days I feel like there is just too much disconnect and the only thing brown about me is my skin. I've lost my mother tongue, my stories, my religion. Some days reconnection feels like too big of task, too much for me to hold. Sharing my art with my chosen family and QT*IPOC has been a monumental part of my healing. I share my art so my stories can be witnessed, so that I can share my truths and my pain. I also share so that other QT*IPOC can see their stories and struggles represented. I have gotten feedback from people who have heard and seen my art, and who have resonated with my words and feelings. This is so powerful. To hear your struggles and art connect to someone's experiences and supporting them is healing for me and for my community. Creating and sharing art with my chosen family have been monumental in helping me start to reconnect with my past, the pain held in my body and my strength and my inner shakti, without feeling so alone in the process. They have been a huge source of inspiration and love for me.

10

Becoming Naz:
Transitioning to My Truth

Naz Seenauth

On October 5th 1994, I was born with my twin sister, prematurely, into an incredibly loving Guyanese-Muslim family. My family was there for me every second from my first breath. My grandmother often tells me the story of how I was born bald, one pound and fourteen ounces, and how the blanket they had me in was heavier than me. She said there were people who thought I would die. My mother tells me that my father spent nights, after working long hard hours, feeding me and trying to get me to burp. And he would rub my back so many times, my tiny little clothes would be worn out. My grandfather used to take us for walks around the block across the street from our house. Regardless of what we were wearing, he'd hold our hands or carry us on his shoulders. And my father used to tie strings to giant diaper boxes and drag us around on them as if we were racing across the world in our living room. My mother is amazing. She would spend every waking moment of her life taking care of us when we were younger. I guess that is why it is said, "heaven lies at the feet of our mothers." She fed us by hand, took on the job of preschool and taught us how to read letters, numbers and Arabic. She is the reason I entered elementary school knowing how to read. Teaching us Arabic made her happy; she wanted us to be pious Muslim daughters who were able to perfectly read the Quran. She had so much patience for us. I was such a pain growing up; I would never sit still. And I was one of those kids who would take things apart and break it in the process of trying to figure out how it worked.

Then at four or five years old, I entered elementary school. I lived across the street from the school, it had a giant playground and after lunch, all the kids would go outside and play. We came up with incredibly creative games running up and down the asphalt. I loved making up these games. One day when I came home, my mother scolded me for playing with the boys. She told me I was a girl and I had to play with the other girls. I didn't understand what she meant by her comments nor did I want to start playing with the girls. I did not understand why I could not play with boys, and I was not interested in playing with the girls. I felt like I related better to the guys. The guys would run around and play rough while the girls would walk around the lot and talk. I wanted to run around but according to my mother, I wasn't supposed to. I felt frustrated because I didn't understand why it was so bad to play with the guys. Instead of listening to her, I continued on playing with the guys, and it was fun for a while until I got a little older.

As a young kid, to be different than everyone else was a major issue. If you dressed without name-brand clothing, spoke with an accent, acted in any way contrary to your prescribed sex or did anything different from the collective, you would be bullied and ostracized. My peers would constantly taunt me. Their teasing would hurt and humiliate me. I was about seven years old when I became friends with a girl and had a bit of a crush on her. She found out about my crush and denounced our friendship. Then she told the entire grade which made their insults worse. I learned the unspoken rule of conformity; I couldn't exist because of the reactions of my peers. And from that moment, I realized that talking about how I felt towards girls or my gender was not allowed.

Even when I said nothing, I was still an easy target because of my naturally masculine disposition. A memory that I've held on to, is one where I was in the auditorium of my school and a girl came up to me and asked as loudly as she could, "Are you gay or a tomboy?" I said "no." I said no, not only because I was ashamed of the question but because I didn't know what it meant to be gay. My family never discussed sexuality and gender. Islam outlined my understanding by telling me men and women were to be separated and I was supposed to get married to a pious Muslim man after college. But even at the masjid, during Saturday Madrassa, I would hang out with the guys and have pizza eating contests and learn how to make beats on the plastic tables. This didn't make many people happy because I wasn't obeying the rules. I was not only mixing with the guys but I was also acting like one.

The obvious disapproval forced me to abandon all of my ways; I was tired of trying to fight everyone in my life. My family, schoolmates and everyone around me wanted me to be more feminine, and I gave in. I made myself pretend to like boys. I told the biggest gossiper in class that, I liked this boy, and she told everyone. Now everyone would think I was more "normal." I also tried to dress more feminine by wearing skirts, colorful clothes and jewelry. Finally I was like everyone else. My peers stopped bullying me and I felt more at ease in the outside world. However, on the inside I felt even more conflicted. I still wasn't really like all of the other girls so I decided to fake it and wait until I became like everyone else.

As puberty hit, I felt as though the world was going to come down on me. My body was physically betraying me; I was developing into a woman. I was uncomfortable, angry, sad and a bit traumatized by my body's changes. I wanted it to stop. I thought every other girl felt the same way and in time, I'd get over it. Instead I plunged into this deep depression and had incredible shame about my body, and I was very self-destructive. My grandmother told me I'd be okay, and menstruating is a part of life. But it never felt okay. I would fight with my body. By not eating, I'd hope my breasts wouldn't grow. I also learned that not eating would stop my periods, so I didn't eat, or I'd binge and purge food. I once made it four months without a period. Then when I did eat, I would work out, run at least two or three miles a day, just so my breasts would stop growing and my periods wouldn't happen as often. Along with all of the incredible discomfort with the femaleness of my body, I was noticing my attraction to other girls my age. And since many people had previously told me my attraction to girls was wrong, I repressed my feelings and continued to push myself to be attracted to boys.

Then at about fifteen, I couldn't handle trying to fit in anymore. I finally admitted to myself I was attracted to women and told a few people. Yet, I couldn't tell my parents. They wanted me to marry a man and have kids. I was supposed to find a nice Muslim boy to marry. In high school, coming out as a lesbian didn't go over too well but I was able to come to terms with my sexuality because there were positive images of lesbians in the media and I knew a few lesbian couples. Even though I was at ease about my sexuality, my body dysphoria came back. I didn't want to become a woman, but I didn't know it was possible to identify outside of one's biological sex.

Becoming Naz: Transitioning to My Truth

I couldn't handle trying to be what everyone else wanted me to be anymore. I decided to be myself by wearing what I wanted and doing what I wanted. I went back to wearing masculine clothing and dating women. For a while, I felt as though a major weight was lifted off of my shoulders, but it didn't last for too long. I used to do a lot of media work within the Islamic community. It felt as though I was doing a great service to my community, but I ended up needing to take a step back because of a hurtful phone call I received from a mentor. She called me and told me I was amazing and made many great contributions. After the pleasant comments, she went on to tell me I was supposed to wear more *salwars* and *jilbabs* instead of men's dress shirts and pants. She said that I had the temperament of an ideal Muslim and great skills that could contribute to the Islamic community but the problem was that I dressed and acted too masculine. If I changed that, I'd be a perfect Muslima Leader. I realized I couldn't stay in a place that limited my freedom to express who I wanted to be. Even though they loved what I did, they didn't love me as I am. So, I walked away in an attempt to understand and figure out who I am, and to live as authentically as possible.

I surfed the internet and found videos online of transmen who had started transitioning. Every few weeks they'd put up videos of their bodies changing and share their endeavors to have top-surgeries. These videos resonated with me, but I refused to admit it to myself. Instead, I kept my internal conflict to myself. It was a great plan, until my inability to come out to myself led to self-destructive actions and suicidal thoughts. I couldn't handle my feelings anymore and desperately needed to resolve this conflict I was faced with. One afternoon, I was lying in bed struggling with these thoughts and decided I had to make a choice. Do I continue suffering and ultimately commit suicide or do I choose to live and struggle but live my truth? I took out my phone and sent a message to my closest friend, terrified because as much as she loved me, she was a Hijabi and she might leave me. I told her "I think I want to be a guy." In that moment, I chose to live. My radical beautiful Hijabi friend told me she would support me by any means. From that moment, I realized I was allowed to live my truth and become the person I was looking to become.

In my senior year of high school, I came out to someone I consider as my second mother. She was the youth development coordinator at school, so she had resources that supported me in the ways my mother couldn't. Instead of just giving me the address, she literally walked me over to a center that helped me in ways I will never forget. The people in the center jump-started my transition process by allowing me to be myself. They made sure the staff knew I preferred masculine pronouns (he/his/him) and introduced me to a community health center that would ultimately help me with physically transitioning. I had all these amazing people in my corner, accepting, helping and loving me. I was on a journey to being my real self and my parents were not aware at all. I considered my choices: I could run away, transition and never come home again or I could face them and tell them that transitioning was what I needed to do. In the end, I did one of the most progressive acts a brown person can do, and consulted a family therapist who agreed to be present when I told my parents. Along with the family therapist, I worked with another therapist who helped me plan every detail of coming out. I decided I wasn't going to tell my parents until after I started taking testosterone because they would have done their best to convince me that I shouldn't transition, and I probably would have listened.

After I turned 18, I started testosterone, wrote a letter to my parents and made sure that if I got kicked out of my house, I'd be okay. I considered every scenario and took every precaution possible. When everything was planned out and I couldn't stall telling my parents anymore, I invited the family therapist to my house on January 10th, 2012. My parents were thoroughly confused but they went along with what I asked. When it came time for me to talk, I couldn't say a word. Even though the letter was there for me to read, I couldn't bring myself to read it to them. I handed it to the therapist and she read it to them. It read:

"Dear Parents,

I know this may be hard to hear but I am transgender. Which if you don't know it means I identify as male. I've known for quite some time, and through a lot of thinking and talking, I made the decision to transition. On November 29th, I got my first shot of the hormone, testosterone, as part of my transition. The shots happen biweekly. So by now I've had 4. This transition wasn't a random decision. I didn't wake up one morning and decide that I wanted to change my sex. I've felt like something was wrong with me my entire life up until I made the decision to transition. I finally feel like a whole human being, whatever was missing has been found. And for me that is a great accomplishment. So I'm telling you of my transition because I want to share my happiness with you. Also, I'm tired of hiding who I am to you. Not letting you know has been a burden, it's felt like living two different lives. I know that I've made this decision without consulting you beforehand but that's because I assumed that you wouldn't be accepting and I needed this to be concrete before telling you. Also, this decision wasn't made under the influence of anyone or anything, this is solely my action. I'm not out to cause shame to our family, I am doing this to feel sane and normal. The only way that felt safe to tell you is to have this therapist here with us. To help process my transition because I need you all to gain some sort of understanding. Right now, I'm not asking you to call me by masculine pronouns or anything of that sort. All I want right now is for you to just gain an understanding of who I am and why I'm doing this. Because hopefully, through understanding, you can gain acceptance or at the very least tolerance. Regardless of the physical changes, I will be the same person at the core. My gender-identity is a small but important aspect. I need you to remember that I will be the same person. I know, in this moment, this may not seem like the right thing for me to do. But in time, I hope you do."

After the therapist read the letter, there was an incredible silence in my living room; I don't think there was ever so much silence in my house. My parents were in shock for a while until the yelling began. I expected the yelling but I couldn't say anything. I was terrified and the therapist asked the one question I was dying to ask: Was I going to be kicked out of the house? My parents said they could never kick their kids out of their house and they still loved me. I started crying. My two biggest fears were that they wouldn't love me anymore and they would kick me out. They didn't do either and I was relieved. They didn't want me to transition, but my life depended on it. I realized they were more afraid than angry. They were making statements along the lines of my life being harder because of my choice. They grappled with the idea that their daughter wanted to be a son. They were in mourning of their daughter. And it made complete sense; for seventeen years they had known me as their daughter. They were allowed to mourn, on some level, they had lost their daughter.

I learned to be patient. I was the one changing on them, and I didn't want to push them too much. After all, they were my family. My grandparents were the first of our relatives to know. When my grandmother found out, I thought she was going to yell at me but she told me as long as I was happy and healthy, it was okay. She thought it was what Allah-willed. My grandfather, this man of traditional values, tried to figure out what pronouns to use and asked how school was going. I was surprised my grandparents took my transition better than my parents. My parents slowly began to come around. They stopped yelling at me about transitioning and they didn't ask about it. They did ask about my health. Presently, although pronouns are an issue, I know my parents and my family will fight for me. It was and still is a process, but I think they've come to realize I am still the child they love, if not even better because I am happier.

Becoming Naz: Transitioning to My Truth

As for Islam, I am struggling with my spirituality, but I've found that often times, the problem is the culture of the community. Many Muslims in my community are trying so hard to be right that instead of propagating true Islamic Muslim Values of peace, love, kindness and humility towards their fellow brothers and sisters, they are condemning each other. Although there is conflict and rejection, I have come across people within the Muslim community, who have accepted who I am. I was able to reconcile with Islam because I realized that religion is your own belief, and no one else can decide or tell you you're not allowed in a religion. It is up to you. So I chose to commit to Islam.

Looking back, if anyone told me five years ago that I would be living as authentically as I am now, I wouldn't have believed them. And if they had told me my family would ultimately learn and accept my truth, I probably would have told them they were irrational. Even though I have struggled and I am still struggling every day, every second of it is worth it. I am forever grateful for my journey because I can get up in the morning, look in the mirror and see a person I am proud to be. I could not have done it without my friends, my support systems, and even though it is challenging at times, I could not have done it without my beautiful family.

11

When it's Easier to Be Queer than Desi

Rukie Hartman

My relationship to Desi identity and community has always felt complicated. I'm an Indian adoptee and was born in Calcutta, India. I was adopted and raised by two white parents, and I have a Korean sister. Growing up, I was surrounded by mostly white people, and I can count all the Desi people I knew on one hand, most of whom were also adopted. It was weird to learn about what it means to be Indian from the perspective of people who didn't have immersive experience of India or Indian culture (friends, family friends, teachers, parents, strangers, etc.) To them, Indian culture meant: Bollywood, arranged marriages and Hinduism, and all of this was encompassed by "Third World." Often these conversations would come up by someone saying, "Are you Indian?" or "I read a book set in India" or "I've always wanted to go to India" or "I once met an

Indian person who…" This was how people thought they could best connect with me, but I never really knew how to respond. I don't blame people for trying to make these connections and to my benefit, these interactions helped spark my own interest in learning about Indian culture.

When I started watching Indian films, I 'learned" about the dynamics of Indian families. Like with many films, some of the representations reflect our own lives while others do not. As a teenager desperate to know anything about Indian culture, I took most Bollywood movies as truth. I learned that Indian culture meant misogynistic, love-stricken men, women and girls having to live within rigid cultural expectations, and gossipy family members treating their kids like playing cards to see who has the best hand. This included pressure on youth to become a doctor, lawyer or engineer, and of course getting married and having babies. In the movies, a person who lacked interest in marriage elicited family fear that they might be lesbian or gay. That accusation would come from a well-meaning but gossipy aunty, and the parents would dismiss it, but remain worried. Most often the accused would not be lesbian or gay, but rather, be interested in someone also not considered an appropriate match because of race, religion, caste, or anything other than sexual orientation. In the end the parents would learn to accept this unconventional love and everything would be okay. These films showed me that unconventional love was okay as long as you weren't actually lesbian or gay. It may seem silly that I would let movies of all things influence my knowledge of a diverse group of people, but as a teenager really wanting to connect with my roots, *why wouldn't I have thought the movies were 100% accurate?*

When I was fourteen, my mom and I took a trip to India to see the sites and visit the orphanage I lived in before being adopted. It was a great trip full of fun memories. In many ways this trip shifted my understanding of Indian cultures and I was able to recognize stereotypes more clearly. Not all men exuded misogyny left and right, some women lived fairly independent lives, and many people we met would discuss cultural stigmas that did not align with their personal values. But even my Mom and her friend, who traveled with us, couldn't help but indulge in a little Bollywood-style gossip. They would make silly remarks such as, "Oh *he* is cute, should I talk to his mother?" (for an arranged marriage). I knew they weren't serious, but in my little queer heart and mind it was super awkward. *I didn't want to marry a boy! But if I didn't want to marry a boy then which Indian person would ever want to be my friend?* Though I had not really thought of myself as queer at that time there was now another insecurity, in addition to being adopted, that would keep the prospect of connecting with Desi community at a distance.

I came out to my family when I was sixteen. I knew my family would not be upset by my queerness because they never said anything judgmental or negative about our family friends who are lesbian or gay. This was enough to know that being queer was okay. My family's support played a big role in my own confidence as a teenager, which made being queer feel easier than being Indian. I didn't have the same worry about someone asking if I was queer like I did if they asked if I was Indian. No one could see my queerness in the way that they could see my brown skin and Indian features. I didn't have to worry about being ignorant on the topic like I did when asked about Indian culture. At the time, I was involved in multiple queer activism projects and could talk extensively about my involvement. Participating in queer activism also helped me feel supported because I met new friends and it provided a way to talk about these issues with my family. In my mind, being Indian and being queer didn't really overlap. I was perfectly okay being the only queer person I knew, who happened to be Indian. The possibility of other queer Indian people in the world never crossed my mind. Bollywood films always made it seem like queer Indians didn't exist. *And if the movies were true I wouldn't be accepted anyway, so I wasn't missing out.* Even my hardcore liberal family would express concern with what it meant to be a queer Indian girl. In my queer-adoptee world, it was understood that growing up in an Indian society would not have offered me many rights. It was a relief knowing I had so much love, safety and freedom in my life to be who I was.

My separation of queer identity and Indian identity did not always work out so neatly. I don't believe that you can easily separate your identities even if it feels natural at some point in your life. This realization came up for me when my high school English class had to watch the movie *Bend It Like Beckham*, as a way to talk about cultural differences. When we got to the part in the film where the topic of arranged marriage came up, everyone in class assumed I would be able to offer some great insight into this matter. Some of them knew I was adopted but others did not. My classmates asked if I wanted an arranged marriage. I said "no" because I didn't want to give people an excuse to talk at length about how *they* could never marry a "stranger." Saying "no" to arranged marriage wasn't just about appealing to my classmates, but also about not wanting to "out" myself as queer just because we happened to be watching *Bend It Like Beckham*. It felt really disheartening to have my mostly white peers critiquing Indian culture and to have my queerness subtly rolled up into the whole experience.

The feeling that being queer was easier than being Indian stayed with me until part way through college. It felt easier up until I started going to a queer people of color discussion group and realized that a lot of people of color struggle to connect with their family and culture because of queerness. It felt easier up until I could admit that I had been ignoring part of my identity by avoiding other Indians. It was easier up until I wondered why I didn't seem to have any brown friends and if I was only ever going to have white friends. It felt easy up until meeting my first queer Indian friend, while working at the LGBTQ (Lesbian, Gay, Bisexual, Transgender and Queer) resource center on campus. I don't even know what I thought having an Indian friend would be like, let alone a queer Indian friend. I worried that I'd be judged for not having Indian parents, for not speaking any Indian languages, and for not understanding cultural references. I didn't expect us to become friends. I thought if we just kept conversations focused on our queer identities that I wouldn't have to go down the road of explaining my way out of all the Desi things I didn't know. It turns out we *both* had a lot of insecurities about being around other Indians. Our queerness made potential friendships with other Desis seem impossible. I'm sure for both of us it was odd and exciting to have a Desi friend who embraced queerness and wouldn't scorn or gossip about queerness as if it were the epitome of shamefulness. I guess that was the real fear: being seen as shameful or maybe that we were being shameless in our queerness.

Our friendship was difficult at times because I was very "out" and didn't have to think twice about where I went or who I was with, but my friend would always have to consider the risks: *Would we run into their parents if we went somewhere? Would we run into someone who knew their parents and would tell them where they saw us? Would we run into someone from high school who would tell their sister, who would tell their parents?* Our experiences with family were so different, and I had such a hard time understanding the need to be so cautious. My friend's decisions were always driven by a *what-will-others-think* mentality and I felt so frustrated when our plans would get ruined, as to not raise any suspicions about our whereabouts. It's not like we were secretly dating and were afraid of being seen by someone. We were just spending time together as friends and it made no sense! I'd often say, "You shouldn't care what your parents think so much" or "You can't please your parents forever." I used to think my friend's life would be better if they just cut ties with their family because that is what I imagined myself doing in their shoes. It took a long time for me to get past my own opinions and general stubbornness to truly support what my friend wanted, which was to stay in contact with their family.

Through this friendship I met other queer Desi friends, and my understanding of Desi people began shifting again. No one hated me for being adopted. No one cared that I didn't speak Indian languages or understand cultural references. We had thoughtful conversations about all the stereotypes and representations in Bollywood movies. My queerness was celebrated, and I realized that I had a lot more to learn about Desis. These friends helped me reconcile a lot of the separation I felt about being queer and Indian. There isn't an exact moment when I felt differently about who I am because it is still a process, I simply remember feeling so small around other people of color. For example, when I started going to queer people of color meetings, it was really hard to engage with conversations about family. If someone shared their latest family drama, everyone would say how they "totally understood" or how "something similar happened with me and my family." I cared about these people and their struggles with family, but I couldn't say I understood or had a similar experience. I didn't know if was okay to talk about my family, so I said nothing. This wasn't an option for long because people in the group would ask about my family. I started by sharing what I always told people who asked about me, "Well, I'm Indian, but I'm adopted, but I was born in India, but my parents are white, so I don't really know much about the culture... Did I mention I have a Korean sister?!" Usually this was enough to satisfy the average person who wanted to know about my life, but not this crowd. And it made sense because they were sharing such vulnerable stories about their lives and trusted that I would reciprocate. Our weekly conversations made me realize that I have experienced a lot as a queer Indian in the world, even if it wasn't always about my family. It was great to talk in depth about these issues for the first time, and now I had this group and a bunch of queer Desi friends to support me.

The majority of my Desi friends have difficult relationships with family because they are queer. Though my friends' lives aren't as dramatic or song-filled as a Bollywood movie, they all seem to echo each other in terms of their families being dismissive of their queerness. I know that not all Desi parents are homophobic, but from my perspective, those who do struggle with homophobia don't seem to see it as a prejudice. Homophobia in Desi communities looks like intentionally not telling your child that queer people exist, telling your kid not to hang out with certain friends because those friends might be queer, and refusing to talk to your child if they come out to you. These are only a few ways in which homophobia happens. My friends tell me how their parents will say something to the effect of, "Do you see anyone else in our community doing what *you* are doing?" So, perhaps their parents consider queerness to be un-Indian and thus questions like these seem to not be hurtful. I feel so upset at this notion. *Being queer doesn't make you less Indian!* I guess when people are unable to recognize another person's experience as different from their own, judgment often overshadows understanding. When I see this happen, the stereotypes that I spent so much time trying to challenge seem true. This has made learning how to support my queer Desi friends around family, a learning curve.

Sometimes I can't even comprehend what grappling with homophobia in this way must be like for both my friends and their families. There must be a lot of worry on both sides of this situation. For my friends there must be a lot of: *How do I tell them I am queer? Will I disappoint them (again)? Do they already know? Should I tell another family member first? How do I know if I am really queer? What would my life be like if I weren't queer? Will I have to live a double life forever? What if they ask if I have been with someone? Will they make assumptions? Will they listen? Would they rather not know?*

What if they stop talking to me? Will they understand how difficult it is to tell them that I am queer?

For my friends' families there must be a lot of: *What does this mean? What will the rest of the family think? What did we do wrong? Will they want to bring their partner to family functions? How can they be sure that they are queer? Why aren't they focusing on more important issues? Does this mean that they will not practice our faith? Who will help us understand all of this? Am I ready to know the answers? Haven't we taught them better? Are they safe? Are we safe? How could someone I have known for so long be so different than I expected?* All of these questions must be flying around without maybe ever being said out loud to each other.

This makes me think about how I used to judge other Desis just as much as I feared they would judge me (for being queer and adopted). Now I can see that my friends' parents must be worried about being judged too (for having a queer child). The irony is that even though their queerness is a difficult topic, my friends also talk about how much they love their families, and how much their families love them. My friends tell me how being a disappointment becomes less deflating over time, but I wish it all happened differently. I wish there wasn't so much fear for them or their families.

When I think about all of these questions that my friends and their families contemplate, my brain races too. There is a sadness I feel for everyone involved. I know that when someone experiences fear it can be easier or feel safer to not bring up triggering topics. I suppose the fact that Desi parents are asking these questions means that love and care is on top of, or underneath, or even side-by-side their fear. My parents have probably asked some of these questions too. Realizing that love and care are still present in these relationships makes it easier for me to hear my friends' stories about family time and time again. Don't get me wrong; the stories aren't always heart-wrenching, but even the happiest stories with family often bring us back to where we ache. I know I offer support to these friends, one queer person to another, but I'm still not always sure how to support my friends around their family relationships. When family and community shape our sense of self it feels hard knowing that some of my friends don't have all the support they need and deserve.

All of this brings me back to my family and how they couldn't be more supportive of me. They support that fact that I am queer. They support the fact that on some issues I take a different stance. They supported my decision to major in Anthropology and Gender, Women and Sexuality Studies. They supported my decision to work at a non-profit food bank and to take a part-time job that aligned with my values. They support me and my partner. I've learned to expect all of this support, so it is hard knowing that this level of family support is what some of my friends can only hope for with their family. While I know that anyone's family can be homophobic and unsupportive, I used to attribute my parents' support to the fact that they are such staunch liberals. I was never really sure what my queer Desi friends would think about my parents. However, I found that when I do tell them about how my partner and I spent the weekend visiting my parents, or how we went out for a birthday dinner, or took a trip somewhere, or went to a family function, my friends always seem so pleasantly surprised. They seem happy that my parents are at ease with my partner and me, and that we can be ourselves in their presence. It feels like my friends take relief in knowing that we are okay at home and happy around my family. I never thought that my white parents could give my queer Desi friends a sense of hope when it comes to being a Desi queer.

This hope comes from the fact that as queer Desis, just like when we share in pain, we can't help but feel a shared sense of joy when family supports us. It is the same as how anyone might share in excitement, achievement, loss, or sadness with someone close. I share the support my family gives me with my friends, and when a friend receives support from their family, I share in that joy too. I have a queer Desi friend whose Mum has been a constant support to him since he came out to her, and when I went to visit him for the first time I really wanted to meet her. We only met briefly because she was on her way to work but when I went to shake her hand, she hugged me! I'm not used to hugging people I meet for the first time, but her hug made me want to hug her back. This was the first time I met a parent of a queer Desi friend, who knew I was queer, and who still wanted to hug me. Her hug reminded me why I am working on addressing my complicated feelings about homophobia in Desi communities. If I ignore those moments when people in our community do support queer Desi people, then I'd be allowing myself to lean on a false belief that allyship doesn't exist in Desi communities. The fact that my friend's Mum hugged me proves that belief is false because I feel her hug is an act of allyship, both to me and to her kid. Though her hug doesn't erase every struggle that queer Desis have with family, it feels like a good start toward making it easier to have conversations about queerness with family and community.

I consider myself pretty damn lucky to have a small pocket of Desi community whose love and friendship have allowed me to unlearn many of the negative stereotypes I once associated with being Indian. As an adoptee, I feel like I could have gone most of my life without knowing much about other Desi people (in part by my upbringing as well as by choice). If this had happened, I might have continued on for many more years than I already had, avoiding other Desis and pretending to be okay. It is these friends, mentors, professors, and even some aunties and uncles who have made being Desi feel easier and less isolating. When it comes to my fellow queer Desi friends, there aren't even words to describe all the ways in which they help me feel whole. I mean, there was probably a time when we all thought we were the only queer Desi on the face of the planet, and yet we managed to not only find each other but also heal parts of ourselves we maybe had to abandon in order to feel validated as queer people.

I wish I could tell my queer Desi friends' parents how amazing and loving and smart and compassionate I think their children are. Maybe if their parents knew that I felt this way there would be less fear. The unique space that I occupy with being queer and adopted allows me to advocate for my queer Desi friends and hold my belief that our families and community can hear what we need them to know over the *what-will-others-think* voice in their mind. Though I'm not likely the person they fear will judge them, maybe it would give them reason to question any judgment. Perhaps they will feel inspired to tell "others" how amazing, loving, smart and compassionate their children are. Even though not all parents know how to support their queer children, I'm learning to hold love for my friends' moms who aren't ready to hug me just yet, because they deserve support too. It might take some time for them to get there and that's okay. In the meantime, we can shake hands, engage in awkward small talk, share in nervous laughter, stare at the wall when there is a long silence, eat snacks and sip chai, ask each other about hobbies and favorites, watch our favorite Bollywood movies and maybe even share in some light-hearted gossip.

12

Coming "In" to Myself

Umar Hafiz

I remember poring over tedious math workbooks with my mother when I came home from school. Later we would tackle biology flashcards and after that, I'd do my actual homework. I'd sit at the dining room table, unable to focus on the work in front of me, wanting to be free. My eyes would wander around the room, first to the clock, mournful of playtime lost, then to my mother who would be flipping through a magazine or reading the mail. They always ended with the delicate snow globes in the china cabinet just past her. These ornaments intrigued me: perfectly shaped spheres depicting equally perfect scenes of happiness, joy and promise. Even when I shook them and introduced chaos into their worlds, something beautiful came of it. My attention snapped back to reality as my mother tapped the table and sharply said, "Beta! You need to learn this." School was the motivation for everything my mother made me do.

I hadn't realized, then, that school was just another stepping stone on the true path my parents had set out for me. I mean, I had always known that I was expected to be a doctor. However, it simply hadn't occurred to me that the supreme value they put on my education was not for the sake of education itself, rather it was simply another stepping stone on the path to a well-paying career. It wasn't the quality of education that was important, rather it was the grades I brought home.

As immigrants from Pakistan who arrived in the U.S later in their lives, my parents saw the world with a different albeit predictable lens. I was to "grow up," have a well-paying career, get married to someone they chose or at least approved of, and start the next generation of children who were to repeat the cycle. It was a fate I accepted, welcomed even – like a zoo animal bred in captivity, I knew of nothing else.

My parents' outlook on the world was obviously a product of their own upbringing. They had conservative ideas of the roles of men and women in society. Men were expected to care for the family by providing income, while women were taught to believe their role was at home raising children. This belief was a societal norm in Pakistan and something my parents accepted without question, likely because it was all they knew, too. Immigrating to the U.S. did little to change their expectations of their own children.

And for the most part, I fulfilled them. Every Sunday I went to Islamic school to learn about Islam and what it meant to be a good Muslim. During the week my mother sat me down every day after school to read a part of the Qu'ran, while I impatiently tried rushing through it to catch my cartoons. Being completely written in Arabic, I was never directly taught about the words I was reading – I just knew that for some prayers, I needed to be able to recite the words. My education, both academic and religious, took a similar path. I was to rote memorize a string of facts. Truly understanding concepts and learning to think critically was not encouraged.

It was easy to fit into this lifestyle. Everything was laid out perfectly in front of me and all I needed to do was to blindly follow. As long as I did as my parents said, I was rewarded with most of the things I asked for. I excelled academically, even won a few Islamic School Quiz Competitions, and managed to fit into the cookie cutter lifestyle of a Pakistani, Muslim son. My life was another one of my mother's snow globes: a perfectly crafted world with a perfectly planned future.

However, as I entered my teen years and took the plunge into puberty, I started to feel something that was...different. At first, I couldn't quite place it. I felt more aware around the males in my life, almost as if I were being more attentive when they were around. While I was at ease around my female friends, I found that I was more concerned with the male relationships I had. I didn't think much of it, though, because I didn't have many male friends growing up. I wasn't very good at or even interested in sports and had always been very shy. As I progressed through middle school, however, it became more apparent that I was attracted to men. This realization was a tremor in my world. It was a crack in the beautifully polished glass my mother had worked on for so many years to perfect.

I didn't know how to process these feelings. Being the one on the inside of the snow globe this time, I realized I never knew how problematic a sudden snowstorm could be. At Islamic school, I was constantly taught to think of homosexuality as "being bad." It was rattled off as just another vice and grouped in the same list as murder and adultery. I was taught about homosexuality from people who had no understanding of human sexuality and it fundamentally shaped my vision of who I was. Peers at both public school and the Masjid always used the word "gay" to describe anything that they thought was stupid or annoying. Internally, I began to believe in these ideas of myself and at a core level I rejected myself on the basis that my attraction to men was inherently bad.

Through navigating my sexual identity, my parents didn't serve as a resource or guide. My father's expectations for my role as his son, and of men and women in general, put a wedge in our relationship early in life. He expected my mother to raise my sister and me, which allowed him to quietly fall to the back seat. We grew up coexisting and cohabitating, but largely as strangers. I was expected to obey him and help him with whatever he needed. And, although I did not revere him as a resource or guide, ironically the one thing I did learn from him was resourcefulness. I remember often spending entire days of the weekend assisting him on different failed projects he'd decide to take up – whether a household fix or something to do with a computer that was beyond repair. My father always made me use the internet to first research the issue and then we'd try to employ any fixes we found on our own. I kept this with me moving forward in always trying to figure things out for myself and solve problems on my own.

This kind of thinking translated into how I dealt with my sexuality. When I first realized in middle school that I was gay, I took to the internet to try and understand what I was going through. Part of what helped me process it were the numerous articles that said such feelings were natural. That many boys went through this "phase" during puberty and eventually it would go away. This information helped me breathe a sigh of relief and shield myself with the knowledge that all would "right" itself in time. It also helped me quiet the storm that threatened to disrupt my life, as if promising to mend the cracks left behind by the realization of my homosexuality.

Coming "In" to Myself

The way I handled difficult situations was largely shaped by how my family handled anything – by keeping up appearances. My father and I would get into intense arguments followed by a silent treatment of each other that would sometimes last months at a time. However, when we were in front of other people, I was expected to look and behave like all was well. Arguments with my mother followed the same trajectory except she often rebounded the next day pretending nothing had happened. I was meant to follow my parents' word without question, and even when I did question things, my thoughts were immediately brushed aside. This practice helped me learn how to manage my emotions, mainly by ignoring them, and made it easier for me to undermine and disregard my own thoughts and feelings. My parents and I couldn't, and still can't, communicate openly with each other because they aren't able to be honest with themselves and with me about our relationship – or really about any uncomfortable truth.

Dealing with my problems in this way cultivated a strong sense of indifference in me. It helped me throw up my guard easily and blot out anything that felt uncomfortable. When I first faced my sexuality, I was able to do what I had always done – sweep it under the rug. The knowledge and hope that this could be a phase made it even easier to do so. Listening to the *khutbahs* (sermons) at the *masjid*, I could hear the messages against homosexuality with a slight grimace and move past them. With so much practice keeping up appearances, I was able to move through life quietly hiding a piece of my identity. I continued to believe that one day I would get married to a woman, raise children of my own, and grow old in the life cycle that was expected of a Muslim boy. I was content to live my life as a series of steps; a neatly laid out path that would get me to where I was supposed to be.

What changed all this, then, was my starting to volunteer in middle and high school. It started off as being yet another thing I was meant to do for resume building and college admissions. But it resonated with me on a deeply human and moral level. I worked on all sorts of projects: helping out at a soup kitchen, participating in walks to cure various diseases, and I even got involved in an advocacy project for child soldiers. Service gave me the opportunity to lend my voice to those who had none – something I was all too familiar with. I carried this commitment to human rights with me to Drexel University and it was there that much of my thinking radically changed.

My time at Drexel proved to be an enormously transformative experience. It began as the next step in the path to becoming a doctor and to becoming the son my parents envisioned and could be proud of. I still lived in their world, their well-polished globe, with minor cracks left behind from my adolescence, but who doesn't acquire a few scars on the way? I was content to pursue a degree in biology and take the classes predetermined for my medical school track which was predestined for me by my parents. I didn't see a reason to stray from the path and so I chose not to.

However, my sexuality, which was supposed to be a "phase," had maintained itself throughout middle school and high school. It was getting harder for me to fit into the cookie cutter lifestyle my parents wanted for me and it was getting harder to be the perfect Muslim son. When I started college I continued to believe that I could do all this, but this idea was slowly and heavily challenged.

It started first when I joined the Drexel Community Scholars (DCS) program, a part-time AmeriCorps program which integrated civic education with community experience. The program provided me with an exposure to deeper reflections on service. The point of these reflections was to push us to think critically about the work that we were doing and to recognize that community service isn't merely "good deeds." Service includes a range of possible emotions and motivations. Additionally, what fuels the need for this service? Why is there a gap in resources for what people need? In essence, my reflections taught me that service is complex, and in order for me to recognize its complexity, I had to be pushed to understand the broader context of social issues as well as the history and policies which fuel the need for it.

The DCS program gave me a space to question anything and everything. It helped me understand concepts of privilege, identity, race and power, and gave me the language to talk about my experiences as a racial and ethnic minority in America. The program connected me to networks of other people with similar experiences, who served as role models that looked like me. For the first time, I had been pushed to think critically about things I had previously thought to be very straightforward. This was the complete opposite of the rote memorization education and "do as you're told" mantras that I was raised with.

And it translated into everything I did.

I could no longer sit patiently through the Imam's *khutbahs* or Muslim community leaders' speeches that viewed the world with a black-and-white, cut-and-dry lens. I remember one sermon where the Imam talked about a homeless man who committed suicide after his dog died. "If only he had one ounce of *deen* (faith) in his heart, then this wouldn't have happened and he wouldn't have committed this sin." But what about the social context in which this man had lived? Given the dehumanizing way society is conditioned to treat the homeless, maybe his closest companion was his dog. Imagine the physical and mental burden he might have struggled through without having any social or emotional support. The lines between black and white were starting to blur and I was starting to see the world for what it is: a spectrum of greys.

This thinking began to sever my ties with the kind of Islam I was used to: one that promoted thoughtlessness and blind obedience. I started to question aspects of the religion I still followed, like only eating Halal meat, for example. What made a cage-raised animal bred inhumanely in a factory farm any more holy than one that was field-raised, just because it was killed a certain way? I was free to question my religion, inquire into it more deeply, and reinterpret the meaning of its teachings in ways that simply made more sense. I discovered that the Qu'ran never really mentions anything about homosexual love – rather it condemns homosexual lust. This thinking was aggravating the cracks in my already tarnished world and threatened to break the glass I had so long been trying to mend.

At the beginning of my junior year, I lifted the rug and briefly revisited my sexuality. Up until that point, I had continued to hide my queerness and tried to believe in myself still following the same path that I was expected to. But I also knew that I wouldn't do someone the injustice of marrying her without being able to fully love her. I quietly made the decision to simply not get married and maybe even try out the single father thing, and tucked the matter away back under the rug it had been hidden under for so many years.

It couldn't stay hidden for very long, though. By that point I had understood what it meant to feel empowered, I just wasn't ready to be honest with myself about how my life was going to proceed. I still clung to the notion of living the cookie cutter lifestyle of the perfect Muslim son. And so, junior year continued normally with me just as involved as ever, both on and off campus. I was still working with the DCS program now leading workshops to help foster critical thought around different topics like poverty, race, wealth and privilege. I brought new students into the service sector and led reflections to try and help volunteers understand both the value and the complexity of what they were doing.

Coming "In" to Myself

A month before the end of the academic year, something one of my closest friends said to me struck a chord and began my ascent into "coming in" to myself and my sexual identity. She was someone who understood and knew me deeply – both on a personal and cultural level. The one thing she didn't know was my sexuality, which had always been the one part of me I kept hidden no matter how close I became with someone. It was always one final thing that I could hide behind – one guard that always remained raised.

I remember sitting in her apartment, telling her about something I did to get back at an inconsiderate roommate. She laughed and scolded me, to which I shrugged and said that I was okay with the morally grey. "Even if you are, you'd feel better in the long run for choosing not to do it…I feel like someone or something along the way convinced you that you are a bad person, but you're not, you *are* a good person."

I shrugged her off and in the moment neither she nor I knew the kind of effect what she had said would have on me. Over the next few weeks, her statement lingered – small at first – a quiet tremor that unsettled some of the snow. But then its presence grew larger and larger in my mind, engulfing it in the snowstorm I had tried to avoid for so long. Why was I okay with the "morally grey"? I realized that at least part of it had to do with my being so easily indifferent. Yet at the same time I felt deeply about so many things – people, causes, events, music. How did I come to be this contradiction of both apathy and empathy?

She was right, along the way something had convinced me I was inherently bad. My sexuality and its relationship with my religion had made me internalize this idea of myself as bad, which made me okay with doing morally "grey" things. I thought critically about my sexuality just like I did about other things like the media or race or even privilege. And just like privilege, I realized that my sexuality was something I had no control over. There was no point in my life where I chose to be one way or another – it just happened. And most importantly, my sexuality did not dictate my morality in the way Muslim leaders portrayed. I really was and tried to be a good person.

My critical thought-inspired education provided the fuel to my liberation, and my friend's statement was the spark that lit the flame. I no longer had to practice Islam taught through the lens of Muslims born into normalized extreme heteropatriarchy. Learning all these concepts and theories helped shift the framework of my thinking and introduced so much mayhem into my world. It shattered the glass of my snow-globe-perfect life, which my mother had striven to cultivate – the same glass that I had tried to live within and mend. Now I can no longer live within the bounds I once tried to and nor do I want to. I can live in a new world, one that is open and open-minded, and in which my choices are my own. Looking back, I realize that amidst the chaos and the rubble left behind, something beautiful has come from it. Now, I am free.

13

Recipes and Rites

Raju S. Singh

Circumstances are always connected.

They always influence and impact each other.

Like my aunt told me when she found out I was transgender:

"There are consequences y'know, beta!"

Those words hurt my ears at the time. Like chili-stained fingers that burnt badly when I tried to block my ears with them. I was not ready to hear those words; I was defensive. But *what about the consequences I have lived with?* I thought to myself. There are consequences I had no choice about – the neglect and abuse I suffered as a child, not having a father growing up, not being able to focus during school years due to trauma, developing a drinking problem and chronic illness, and facing discrimination on so many levels along the way.

Growing up in this harsh white Western world was hard enough for a brown adolescent like me let alone paired with not having the love I needed and deserved. *What about those consequences?!*

So, consequence? Impact? Influence?

All three exist in my life.

It has been a couple of years since *they* 'found out.' I'm talking about my family of origin, namely my mother and older brother, a cousin, and a couple aunts. My mother had guessed from the careless, unintentional clues I left scattered around her shattered dreams. She picked them up, googled me, found a zine I was writing and discovered my deepest thoughts that I put out there on a blog for the world to read, hoping someone out there in cyberspace could relate, and would respond.

Well, now I can actually feel those consequences my aunt was talking about. My aunt, who was really my mother's best friend but had become part of our family displaced in the diaspora. My aunt, who had saved us from our father, who had been a second mother almost, and who had supported us through hard times and had always guided me. She had done so much that I was just as scared to disappoint her as I was my mother. I remained in a state of constant anxiety around them both and the rest of the family growing up. The only way I found to get through it all was to be silent, whilst in my activist life, I was uncensored, forever speaking and advocating about gender and sexuality. This contradiction was difficult to swallow and digest.

I hadn't envisaged it happening this way; I guess I just got caught up in claiming my identity after destructively suppressing it for so long. I had made a decision a few years ago to stop living my life for other people and to live for myself instead, and look what happened?!

Those instances were so connected, just like a recipe in which you cannot make the final meal unless all the ingredients come together, and one ingredient cannot do without the other. You can substitute, but it's not quite the same. The kind of recipe my mother likes to make meals with, the kind we have bonded over making together since I can remember. You know, you add the salt and only then you start to taste all the flavours properly. Y'know, the longer you leave it, the better it starts to taste. The less you handle it and interfere with it and the more you let it do its own thing, the tastier it is in the end. Y'know. Y'know what I'm saying?

I realised that all my experiences, like dot patterns, just needed to be connected to create the whole picture. Every ingredient vital to that recipe. I couldn't live with myself otherwise. Incomplete. Leaving parts of myself at my mother's front door to collect on the way out with my package of leftover home cooked food. I couldn't live up to anyone else's expectations of me either, though I knew that my mother had done so herself in her life, like so many other self-sacrificing South Asian women. This acknowledgement was painful to accept, so I hid from myself for too long, smothered myself by numbing every part of myself that I could feel. But eventually I had to resurface, breathe, feel and be in the world.

Who would've thought that a mother finding out that her daughter chooses a different name than her given one, uses a masculine pronoun and wants to look 'male' rather than 'female,' could actually have something in common with her child in this transformation? This is how she perceived it. How could I tell her I was still feminine in spite of the transformation, that I still wore the suits and shawls she gave me? How could she possibly understand the complexity and contradiction when we

159

grew up in such a gendered community with so much pressure to conform to one gender or the other? My gender felt much more complex than that. I had never fully subscribed to one or the other, not as a child and not as an adult either. My mother thought she had lost her daughter and she didn't want to gain another son. She already had one who fit the perfect son mould, like a personally tailored suit, as opposed to a store bought one that doesn't fit quite right, especially across the chest and the crotch. She was perfectly happy to have one son and one daughter, an ideal deal. It was a shock, a recipe gone wrong, or a recipe for disaster, as they say. Though now, I could wear a men's *kurta* and no one would ever know the difference.

Nothing would make me her 'son,' though she does stumble on calling me 'daughter' these days. I'm not sure if how she regards me even matters to me anymore. Spending time with her is all that counts these days. Losing most of my family has made me realise why spending time together is much more important than any word or label.

We have been meeting up regularly, after a necessary break, coming up with recipes which we make together, mostly so we don't have to talk. No awkwardness, just distraction in a shared interest. That works. Talking would be too much, so we cook, a maternal legacy. I somehow subconsciously instigated this pattern so that we could spend time together in a way that isn't stressful or uncomfortable for us both. I'm mostly learning her recipes but also trying new things that we have both wanted to try, like delicate *dosas* and perfectly round *gulab jamans* that we devour greedily afterwards.

I failed to mention, my mother is an amazing cook. I know that's what they say about all South Asian mothers, but it's true. She could make the tastiest meal you've ever eaten, cooking whilst watching an Indian soap at the same time, and you know the level of concentration needed for that, right? There was a time I used to think she was not such a good mother after all that we had been put through as kids. I know she felt the guilt too, but dammit she knew how to make the most amazing meal and put it on the table whilst working full time. She fed us well and gave us a roof over our heads. *Isn't that what parents are supposed to do?* After all, she did it on her own, single-mother-handedly, with some help from us raising ourselves, so how could I criticize her parenting, even if in the West, this standard is not considered good enough? She did what she could in her situation.

I've been getting to know my mother as a whole person. She's not just my mother, she is a woman with her own life and experiences. It's funny it took this big drama of her realising *my* identity for me to learn this and learn about *her* identity. And with this learning comes the necessary acceptance and understanding for her choices and their consequences.

So the thing about a recipe is that you need to know what you are going to make before you make it. You need to have the ingredients and you have to measure them. My mother never measured anything. It's a bit of this masala here and a bit of that masala there. It's all about the instinctive 'know-how,' learned traditions, the careful tasting and the acute attentiveness. I used to wish that she could have given me that same attention but it seemed that she couldn't hold it steady on her spoon. There wasn't a spoon big enough for what I needed anyway, and she was just too busy or too tired at the end of her long day. Yes, me the Indian daughter who was never as important as the son, my brother, who got most of my mother's attention, whilst I silently acted out. If we were two types of spices, he was definitely the chili, boldly manifesting his presence wherever tasted and I was the salt, I'm right there in front of you, *hello can you see me?* You know I'm there, but I'm in the background, enhancing the other flavours, invisible and ignored.

My brother could not handle what he heard the day he 'found out' about me. He denied it saying, "But she is so feminine, she can't be." I could not believe his denial at first, when we were always playing together with the rest of the boys and tomboys, usually Cowboys and Indians or Ninjas, when our girl cousins openly refused to play with me because I was 'a boy' since I also wanted to paint my nails with them. Then I realised, just like salt does to the other flavours, my femininity enhanced his masculinity. How could he be masculine against my masculinity? He needed my femininity to be masculine. Is this why he used to feminise me growing up, whilst simultaneously protecting and policing me about dating boys? Once I realised this, well I would like to say I felt better, but not really. It was too late and before I knew it, we hadn't spoken or seen each other for a year, just like that. Suddenly I was 35 and he was 37. We were not kids anymore, stubbornly ignoring each other until one gives in or one gets bored and it's time to start a new game. No, we were adults and had been to hell and back together. So, *how could we be so easily torn apart?* I remember how he used to take the blame when we got in trouble so that I wouldn't get beaten by our father, which inevitably meant we *both* ended up getting punished double in the end. I contemplated this many times, often scratching my new found beard with turmeric stained fingers and remembering how I used to love stroking my father's beard when I was a little 'girl,' despite being afraid of him.

Something dawned on me one day at the Desi grocery, whilst picking out the dark green chilies from the basket of various shades, ranging from lime to spinach green with some orange misfits, like me, along the way. My mind wandering while fondling the smooth firmness of the onions and checking the ripeness of the tomatoes with a delicate squeeze, like my mum had always instructed. A thought suddenly came to my mind while pondering the recipe of the day that I was craving; it was a favourite for both my brother and me. This place, a haven sinking in the sea of white – *gora* – gentrification, always reminded me of them. I needed my family, yes, but not just any family, I wanted a supportive one! I needed them warts and all, mouldy patches or not.

I couldn't discard them like the bruised vegetables I was tossing aside, trying to find the best of the bunch for my one-person lunch. I wanted to make that recipe that we shared, the one we both loved. I wanted to call him over and say bhai, let's make peace and break a piece of this *aloo paratha* and dip it in the *dahi* and guzzle it with our pride. I could smell the fond memories; running into the kitchen after waking up to the smells of the *paratha* my mother was frying on the griddle, drenching them with ghee, Panjabi style! But my brother's lime-sharp words came back to me once more as I threw some into my basket, a sour reminder. *'You're killing our mum'* ricocheted repeatedly in my head until I had to leave the store and run down the street gasping for fresh air, bashing perfectly chosen vegetables and squashing the *dhania* in my rush.

But there was no where I could run away to, even when I lived across the city from them, or travelled far away; they were still embedded on my mind like the patterns on my mother's favourite *salwar kameez*.

I needed my family because they were the only ones who knew what we had been through together and survived together. We had a deep dark secret that was too much to confess to others, who wouldn't understand or would brush it off in the normality that patriarchal violence has become in our communities. We understood each other in a way that no one else could, with what we had witnessed and experienced, even though we didn't really know each other anymore. Blood brothers or something; only he would never accept me as one, as his. I would always be his sister even when I stopped looking like one. *Maybe that's why he didn't want to see me anymore?*

Another year went by and I made friends with other brothers and sisters who weren't blood but chosen, like bananas sharing a bunch rather than peas in the same pod. I met other queer and transgender Desis, ready or ripening, like me, and it partly filled that aching gap, that hungry belly yearning to be fed and filled. I was lucky to have met them, whilst travelling, over the internet or in my city, and it helped me reconnect with my Desi culture that I had once discarded due to experiencing fellow South Asians around whom I had felt unwelcome and excluded by, on account of not fitting in and being 'different.' That went for white folks too, who did the same and often there was nowhere to turn. Though it became easier to discard my culture and find a white queer space to hide in, all the while standing out like a sore thumb, I was either hyper visible or invisible. Inevitably parts of me got sacrificed in the process and I was always leaving pieces of myself in different places, almost forgetting myself behind.

Once I began to notice my failure to camouflage and fit in white dominated spaces, I started noticing that there were plenty of Desis and people of colour just like me who also felt the same, with that same awkward look on their faces. Our eyes met and there was no looking back! I longed to show my brother, who had told me what I was doing was 'against my culture.' *See, you're wrong!* I also learned, through educating myself, that there was a huge legacy of people like me in South Asian culture: Kothis, Hijras, tirungais and more. I became politicised, learning that Western colonisation had eradicated many non-Western cultures and with them their practices, including gender and sexual variations that existed long before 'Western civilisation'. I even made a trip to South India to meet people from proactive trans activist communities, swapping stories accompanied by the sweetest chai and sumptuous street food. Many of these people I met I now consider comrades, if not family. The chai in India definitely reflected the trip's sweetness. I mentioned my journey and experiences in India to my aunt and mother via a blog I wrote whilst there and they both responded:

> *'It is always good to be amongst like-minded people, as that nourishes the soul and at the same time provides a good support network. It is important to be who you are and at the same time ensure you are safe and well and happy.'*

> *'Good to know that you have spent time with like-minded people...I gather you found it very useful in your own personal journey and this is important. My concern is always going to be your wellbeing, safety and happiness and whatever aids in that direction is good. I have my own journey... to fully come to terms with it all and am working on that. God is great and looks after us all.'*

I remember being unsure about whether to send my travel journals to them in the first place, hovering above the send button on the computer monitor for several seconds, being coerced only by the heat in the sweltering internet cafe which dampened my doubt and seized my capacity to think sensibly. All I could think about was quenching myself with cold *lassi*. Their responses surprised me at the time, though I was high on adventurous travel antics. Re-reading them on my return 'home' from the 'homeland,' which I now considered a new home, made me so thankful and relieved but also perplexed as to why they could never ever say these words to my (changing) face but could only write them. There's something compelling and potent about words on a page. They can change your life forever and my life was definitely transformed upon my return.

I reunited with my mother and I noticed I was not the only one changing. She had changed her tune too. Fine tuning recipes often involves changing things around a bit and freshening them up with a new ingredient now and then, so my mother says. Her previous *'I cannot call you by your new name or he'* and *'please don't grow a dar'* became a subtle, understated flavour in our changing relationship in which she had been trying in her own way. I had made a promise with myself when my mother found out that I was transgender, that I would be patient and make sure that any changes happened while she was around, and also that we would always be in contact no matter how hard it was. That paid off in many respects, despite the hardship and anxiety of it all. I knew my gender was too complex for her (and many others) to understand at first but I also knew that if we were in close proximity she would soon start to figure it out as it unfolded. She did get more comfortable when she realised I was not turning into a freakish monster, but that I was actually pretty much the same person she always knew. It also meant that she was actually getting to know me better, even though she was too frightened to get to know who I really was for fear of finding out something she didn't want to know. At least she wanted me to be happy with myself.

My mother had said she would never disown me, that she loved me. She also said many hurtful things along the way that I conveniently made myself forget. I had to. Just as I had blocked out much of my childhood abuse. That was the only way I could live with myself, with her and with our shared past. Some recipes just don't need to be eaten and some have much more complex flavours than others, which can be difficult to taste. She got used to my changes. They didn't come suddenly like a shaky hand spilling too much masala in the food. I made sure the changes were blended in nicely and slowly, one at a time adding more and more until the recipe was improving. A good recipe takes time and care after all.

I won't forget the time I went round to her home after not visiting for a long time and only meeting outside her home, because my brother still lived with her and I didn't want to face him. Once he moved out I felt more comfortable, and like a typical home-loving mother she just wanted me to 'come home,' so I pushed myself and obliged. We made some food together again and I taught her how to make alternative to wheat, spelt *rotis*. I think it was *aloo baingan*, one of my favourites and I devoured it in what felt like seconds. She was happy; that role wouldn't change, regardless of gender. I would always be there to eat her food and forget to tell her how good it was on account of enjoying it too much. She would pretend to be annoyed and I would make a silly joke *'mum, it's not as good as last time but I'm sure better than next time'* and she would pretend to hit me with the rolling pin.

Later, on the train home, memories of my father beating us harshly for not eating everything on our plates would creep into my head. Good times with family were always conjuring up other not so fond memories. I'm sure that's how trauma works, reigniting itself like the gas stove that we griddled the *rotis* on earlier. It's difficult to not get burned in the process.

Eventually, thoughts about how I was looking more and more like my father, given the testosterone hormones I took, haunted me. I couldn't bear to look in the mirror, obsessing about whether my mother noticed, whether that was why she didn't want me to grow that beard. If that was why she didn't want me to look or be male, just like her abuser, my father. *Why couldn't I look more like her?* I wept. My partner would tell me I was handsome, my friends would compliment me on how good I looked in my transition, but that didn't help then. Though it did in the greater scheme of things. It helped me love myself eventually and oddly enough, it also made me address the trauma of my past abuse. I began to accept that even if I looked more like my abusive father, that I was very much like my mother and shared the same traits, including not just culinary skills but also emotionality, which she passed down to me along with her secret flavours. She had raised me after all.

I started to look at myself with pride and confidence and began accepting the changes myself, changes that I was also having some difficulty with, even though I was simultaneously enjoying a lot of them. My so called 'transition' was not fast food; quick, comforting and reliably satisfying, but more like a full-course meal, never knowing if all the courses would work together or what flavours were coming next. Having to stop for breaks before each course and yearning eagerly but patiently for a sweet dessert, though it always seemed a long time coming, even as it got closer.

Still, I liked the way I was beginning to look, which I thought represented me better and how I always imagined I looked on the 'inside,' until I would usually catch my own reflection in a mirror, window or even a photograph. Now I could stare back, wave, say hello, and smile. Most of all I loved my new name. I had gotten rid of my abuser's name and with it some baggage, and chose one that fit with my newly embraced Sikh identity, 'Singh.' I kept my first name as my middle name, in honour of my mother who had named me, an accommodation she appreciated, and I gave myself a new first name, Raju. I had been using Raju as a nickname for a while, named of course after my favourite Indian film actor Raj Kapoor whose character sang:

Dhul ka ek badal albela niklaa hoon apne safar me akela
A free spirit I am, humble but joyous. I set out alone on my journey
Chup chup dekhu mai dunia ka mela
I am a silent witness to this carnival of life
Kahe man kare abhiman kare mehman tujhe ik din to hai jana
What use is pride? What use is vanity? You are a guest here and must leave some day
Dafli utha aawaz mila ga mil ke mere sang prem tarana
So raise your voices and your tambourines and join me in this celebration of love
Mera naam Raju gharana anam
My name is Raju and my home is without a name

After I legally changed my name I would annoyingly sing this to everyone, including those who didn't get the reference and thought I made it up myself. Soon after, I began to grow hair, everywhere, including my head and decided to start wearing a pagri (turban) since I had always longed to wear one like my grandfather. My mother kept buying me clothes but switched to shawls and less gendered garments and I loved her for the subtle acknowledgements that she would never be able to speak. Actions do speak louder than words, though I still longed for her words of affirmation.

The more I embraced my Desi culture the more I eased into my identity; it actually made more sense, especially with accepting my femininity alongside the masculinity. Comfort and confidence draped around me with my favourite shawls. My protection from the phobic world.

One day, my mother's husband, a fellow Sikh *pagh* wearer with a talent for making *daal*, showed me how to tie a *pagh* Kenyan style, while my mother watched on, interfering and telling him how to do it better, just as she does when he makes *daal*. We began talking about turbans and my mother's father, my grandfather who wore one, whom I never really knew as he died when I was young but would gaze at in black-and-white nostalgic photographs – big, strong, powerful, with a kind and honest face. An abundance of stories from the past unfolded. We spoke about Kenya and the migration of Sikhs to East Africa, tracing our families back to the Panjab where our ancestors were from. I asked many questions: why they came to East Africa, where they were from in Panjab and before that, names of them all. Some of which my mother couldn't answer and I realised how much had been lost and buried and just how important storytelling was in knowing yourself.

I wanted to know more about my grandmother and her stories and didn't really know anything about her at all or any of my fathers' family either. I wondered how I could know myself without this information.

So I persisted. I began looking at rare, old photographs of my family. There was one in which my tall grandfather was standing next to my short grandmother sitting down and I revisited a memory I had long forgotten from when I was four, just before they died, watching my giant grandfather eating full size Panjabi *rotis* whole! And my little grandmother sneaking sweets to me in secret, with her warm, smiling face.

Cooking food and wearing Indian clothes became a gateway to opening doors to a traumatic, silent past that we had never spoken about. I will never forget the cross-generational conversations that unfolded with the cloth and the creases they contained. By remembering unwritten-only-spoken-recipes, we talked about exactly where and when they were made and eaten, at various family functions through time and space, which led to even more family stories. I began to reflect on how these recipes remained almost the same despite considerable change of countries and their climates. An anchor grounding us in immense migratory change? There had been some modifications though, due to sourcing and local ingredients available as well as cultural fusions, picking up new flavours along the way. Inevitably we did that with ourselves too, picking up our own individual tastes that became reflected in our traits, though we still yearned for our favourite dishes at family gatherings that brought us all collectively together again.

Learning about my ancestors and finding out more about myself in the process, I wound the cloth round and round my head so that it fit, tightly and neatly pointed and proud. For a moment everything fit just as nicely. My family seemed proud and pleased, or relieved, that they were not losing me to bankrupt Western ideals and that I was embracing our own.

At least for a magical moment.

Tonight, as I stir the *daal* I make for Diwali dinner, that I spend with another runaway Desi queer who was disowned and reunited with their family years later, I think of my family and our journey and our special moments. As we sit amongst the feast of foods I've been learning to make with my mother, I think about the trials and tribulations getting here to this point. All the flavours; the amount of hurt and pain, the anxiety and depression, the isolation and fear, the love and narratives and beautiful moments I could not have anticipated or combined together myself. All those ingredients interacting with each other in their very own recipe.

The journey is not over yet; there is still much more work to do and more to learn and room to grow. I'm working on improving this recipe, knowing it isn't perfect. I may not have the exact ingredients I need to make what I want, but I can freestyle with what I have, just the way my mama taught me to.

Biographies, Dedications and Gratitude

Rajat Singh

Rajat is a first-year Indian American living in New York, where he is pursuing graduate study in sociocultural anthropology at The New School for Social Research. He is committed to writing as a form of curative labor, as well as a meditative exercise in introspection. This is his first published essay.

Sasha Duttchoudhury

Aparajeeta, also known as Sasha, is a writer (and reader) who is interested in storytelling through the languages of personal narrative, fiction, poetry, comics, graphic novels, and those moments of oral storytelling that happen over a cup of chai. Sasha sees storytelling, reading and writing, as less of an escape and more as a way of exploring, experimenting, experiencing, enjoying and engaging with worlds in us and around us.

Dedicated to:

Amlan, Meenakshi, Amreeta, Rukshana Hartman-Thomas and Anu Taranath

Gratitude to:

Shahana and Shirin of Flying Chickadee, South Asian Americans Leading Together (SAALT) and the 2014 Young Leaders Institute participants,

Sheri and Russ, Gita, Alix, Uma, Ammara, Anil, Arunima, Leah Lakshmi Piepzna-Samarasinha, D'lo, South Asian artists of all disciplines who have dared to create, and Queer and Transgender South Asians everywhere. Last but not least, thank you to all of the contributors of this project, who trusted us and honored us with their stories.

Alina Bee

Alina is a recovering Pakistani Burger Bachi. She spends her time trying to unlearn unhealthy self-concepts, guilt, abusive and enmeshed family dynamics, academic pathology and queer stigmas. She is relearning to trust and value the embodied experience with the fullness of radical love and understanding. Her interests include cooking, holistic health, making art, competitive sports, reading about trauma, love, diaspora and queerness, writing, and learning about how families negotiate radical love for each other. Alina's current goals are: find more healing and restorative recipes, learn to understand and tell stories with fidelity to the origin, love all her friends and family with as much honesty and resilience as possible, better recognize where boundaries are needed and keep creating and finding community.

Gratitude to:

Marjaan: For never fading, running or leaving. For loving and teaching me love. My brother: For always being there. For being conscious, accountable and loving. For listening. For being resilient. My grandparents: For being unrelentingly gentle and inspiring in everything you all were and are. Rukie and Sasha: For creating this space. For being supportive, understanding and consistent. For asking questions and staying accountable. My cohort: For all your feedback, time and love. My ex: For reframing my becoming with more love. Thank you all.

Bish Pleez

Bish loves storytelling; he dreams of using it to create lasting change in society. He currently uses it in his science outreach, community activism and LGBTQ advocacy. He loves using science to understand how the world works. He has a tendency of over-committing to impossible schedules, and overindulging when faced with an Indian buffet. He loves film. He often wishes his life were a Bollywood movie and he could intermittently break into song and dance. He loves movement. He dances in drag sometimes, to fuck with gender binaries and societal stereotypes. He believes that we need to have more conversations in the South Asian diaspora to eliminate the stigma related to mental health issues.

Dedicated to:

Ma.

Gratitude to:

Teddy for teaching me a better way to love, Staci for helping me understand, Miguel for making me see, Sdd for giving me the opportunity to take back my life, Bdd for raising me. And thank you Kd, NanD, Sunny, Sash and Marquis for your friendship at crucial points of my life.

J. Krishnan

J. is an innately timid creature. She loves genuine interaction with others and thrives on friendships. She is an artist by birth and excels in many artistic arenas. By trade, she is a musician, but by job, a firefighter. Hopefully someday, she and her princess in shining armour can be together, openly, in an accepting environment. As a Soldier there's one thing that J. believes in, it is relentlessness. Goals are achievable, dreams are within reach; all you have to do is get it right, get the fight....and those milestones will be yours. Fight. Win. Get what you deserve.

This step into an unknown world is dedicated to my baby sister. She has been the rock I needed before I even knew I needed it. She is mentally strong beyond her age, and didn't even hesitate to accept my queerness after I came out. Tweedle, you mean the world to me, and I can't even begin to explain what your support means to me. You are my best bud forever and always. I love you, kiddo.

Zain M.

Zain M. is a trans* radical muslim Desi femme identified guy living on Unceded Coast Salish Territories. He is a storyteller and poet and is also exploring the visual arts of performance, film and photography. He believes in storytelling as a powerful medium in all of its forms and cannot wait for this book to be launched and for people to have access to it.

Gratitude to:

Those who stand with us - my Desi queer & trans families and allies, my QT*IPOC (Queer, Transgender, Indigenous and People of Colour) communities, my trancestors and the sick and disabled communities I am a part of. You helped me write this.

To all of the writers who contributed – thank you for sharing such sacred stories. For sharing such vulnerable and beautiful pieces of you, thank you so much. To the organizers – thank you for making time and space for us to have a platform and medium in which our stories can be read and distributed. This gives me so much love and hope for future Desi queer &

trans folks. To the readers, thank you for absorbing these stories and holding them sacredly with you.

Kurangu Paiyan

Kurangu Paiyan is a queer nonbinary Desi who hopes for a revolution that will include their mother. They spend a lot of time thinking of ways to turn their feelings into art. They enjoy being surrounded by other queer and trans people of color, radical POC community, and other people who try to love fiercely and without apology.

Gratitude to:

Sasha and Rukie for creating this space and supporting me through the writing process. Thank you to my Mother, who might not understand, but remains one of my biggest inspirations for love and strength. Thank you to the amazing friends and community that surround me.

Jotika Chaudhry

Jotika is a Queer, Femme, working class, Brown, woman whose roots are in Fiji and Northern India. She was born and raised as a settler on land that was stolen from the xʷməθkʷəy̓əm ((Musqueum)), sḵwxwú7mesh ((Squamish)), Stó:lō, Burrard and Tsleil-Waututh peoples. She is a singer, writer, mixed media artist, listener, an Introvert, an HSP, Community Organizer and aspiring Social Worker. Creating different forms of art is something that has sustained, nourished and kept her alive. Her song poems and writing center around her ancestors' stories of struggle, her stories of diaspora, inter-generational trauma, decolonization, survival and working towards healing trauma to name a few. Her visual artwork aims to bring visibility, and center stories of struggle and triumph for QT*POC. ((Queer and Trans* Indigenous People of Colour)). Her aspirations are to incorporate art as a tool for healing into the work she is doing as a social worker and within her community organizing. To connect feel free to email her at Jotikart@gmail.com

Gratitude to:

Sasha and Rukie, for working so hard on this project and being so supportive throughout the journey. Mom I love you, you raised a strong, creative woman. Zain my Desi femme brother what would I do without you <3. Lydia my dreamboat, you show me how deep love can be. Mateo my warrior brother you inspire me every day. Aly my radical brown punk sibling, I love you. My QT*IPOC chosen family: Firas, Anna, Amanda, Ash, all the radical QT*IPOC folks who fight to survive and thrive you all help me keep going. Shout-outs to my nieces Tamya and Kadija and my sister Julie – you all teach me so much, I love you. My ancestors I feel you, I'm listening. Thank you.

Naz Seenauth

Naz is a first generation Guyanese-American Queer Trans guy based in New York City looking to create positive change in a world of constant struggle. Currently, he is a student pursuing dual undergraduate degrees in Criminal Justice and Culture and Deviance Studies at John Jay College of Criminal Justice. He is a mentor, an educator and a self-proclaimed social justice activist. He aspires to live with authenticity while pursuing all endeavors that come his way. When asked to describe himself, he often says, "I'm just a regular guy with an alternate experience who is trying to learn something each day while understanding what it truly means to live and grow in this strange world and maybe reach enlightenment."

Every queer person from the South Asian Diaspora and their families. We are all struggling but I have confidence that we will survive and thrive. This is for my beautiful family, I know you don't understand me at times, but I am thankful for your efforts and love you all. And for my circle of people, there are too many names to mention but you know who you are, your support has empowered me to become my best self. I am honored to have such amazing people in my life.

Rukie Hartman

Rukie has been brought to this anthology by her eagerness to engage in queer activism in a new way. Being able to create community across the diaspora, and help facilitate writing and sharing stories has been a fun adventure. Since graduating from college in 2013, she has contributed to another book project, *T.I.P.S. to Study Abroad: Simple Letter for Complex Engagement*, which is a collection of letters written alongside her study abroad classmates who traveled to Bangalore, India. She has also written about issues relating to transracial adoption on her personal blog, *No Lotion 4 These Legs*.

Gratitude to:

Sasha for inviting me to be a co-editor on this project. My family, Sheri, Russ and Emily, who are always supportive of my endeavors. And all my friends who have supported and encouraged my work with this project: Anum, Zain, Anu, Rebecca, Gita, Uma, Alix, Hel, Jenn, Stephanie, Laura, and Christina.

Umar Hafiz

Umar is a queer, Muslim activist currently living in New York City. He is working towards his Masters of Public Health degree at Columbia University. Umar stumbled onto this anthology in much the same way he stumbled onto his own empowerment: by a wonderful coincidence. Umar believes in engaging communities of color in empowering and informative dialogues about identity through storytelling. He believes in the healing nature of these stories and wants to disseminate them far and wide for queer youth of color.

Gratitude to:

My friends, a.k.a. my chosen family: Thank you so much for supporting me through the process of finding myself and becoming comfortable in my own skin. To Seth: thank you for creating the DCS program which largely fueled my empowerment and unlocked my ability to think critically about everything. To Hera: Thank you for the spark that started it all and for loving all parts of me. To Aimee: Thank you for giving me the nudge I needed and for loving me unconditionally. To Christie: You know. And to Juliet: I'll tell you later. Finally, Sasha and Rukie: Thank you so much for creating this project, allowing me to be a part of it, and for supporting me throughout the writing process.

Raju S. Singh

Raju is an interdisciplinary artist, creative-critical writer and QT*IPOC (queer, trans* intersex people of colour) community organiser who is proactive about carving space, self-representation and self-empowerment using art and activism to forge creative survival. Based in London UK and working beyond, they are interested in the role of art in social change and transformative healing justice.

Dedicated to:

My mother, for her unbelievable strength through struggle and for the maternal legacy, along with my dear aunts.

Gratitude to:

Nika, for immense insight, friendship and heart. My comrades in London, Berlin, South India and North America for fierceness, creative survival, courage and nourishment. Rukie and Sasha for this important project and the anthology cohort for sharing, providing insight and making this project what it is, powerful.

Made in the USA
San Bernardino, CA
19 December 2018